Tributary Territory
Resigned Territory
Yao = Half independent Aborigines of China
Capitals of shêng (provinces)
" " fu (prefectures)
" " chih-li-chou (districts)
" " chih-li-t'ing (")
" " hsien (subdistricts)
" " chou (")
" " t'ing (")
Towns with more than 500000
more than 100000 Inhabitants.
Chên-chiang (1861) = Treaty Port with Date of Customs Opening
Lamaist Monastery
Selsen-khan
Chahar
Dolon-nor
Chang-chia-k'ou, Kalgan
Hsüan-hua
Ch'êng-tê, Jehol
Ch'ih-fêng
Harazin
Naiman
Liao-ho
Fou-hsin
Chao-yang
Sui-yüan
Ta-t'ung
Shun-t'ien-fu, Peking
T'ien-chin, Tientsin (1861)
Ch'in-huang-tao
Gulf of Chih-li
Shêng-ching, Mukden
Ch'ang-ch'un
Chi-lin
Hun-ch'un (1910)
Lung-ching-ts'un (1910)
Ch'ang-t'u
Hai-lung
Tung-hua
Niu-chuang
Ying-k'ou
K'ai-p'ing
Ning-yüan
Kuan-tung-chou (Russian 1898-1905, Japanese 1905)
Ta-lien (Dairen) (1907)
Lü-shun, Port Arthur
Têng-chou
Yen-t'ai, Chih-fu (1867)
Wei-hai-wei (1898 to England)
Ning-hai
Mouth of Huang-ho
Lai-chou
Ching-chou
Chi-nan
T'ai-an
Yen-chou
I-chou, Lan-shan
Shantung
Chiao (1899)
Kiaochow (1898 to Germany)
Tsingtao
Yellow Sea
Chên-nan-p'u (Chinnampo)
Han-ch'êng (Söul)
Chi-wu-p'u (Chemulpo)
Ch'ün-shan (Kunsan)
Mu-p'u (Mokpo)
Fu-shan
Ma-shan-p'u
Chao-hsien = Corea
Chi-chou I. Quelpart I.
Huang-ho
Imperial Channel
K'ai-fêng
Hsü-chou
Huai-an
Kiangsu
Yang-chou
Chên-chiang (1861)
Chiang-ning, Nanking (1899)
Su-chou (1896)
Shang-hai (1854)
Sung-chiang
Chia-hsing
Ting-hai
Hang-chou (1896)
Shao-hsing
Ning-po (1861)
Anhwei
Lü-chou
Wu-hu
An-ch'ing
Huei-chou
Han-k'ou (1862)
Han-yang
Wu-ch'ang
Sha-shih (1896)
Yo-chou (1899)
Chiu-chiang, Kiukiang (1862)
Po-yang
Nan-ch'ang
Chekiang
Chin-hua
Ch'u-chou
Wên-chou (1877)
T'ai-chou
Ch'ang-sha (1904)
Hsiang-t'an
Kiangsi
Chi-an
Kan-chou
Nan-an
Fukien
Yen-p'ing
Fu-ning
San-tu-ao (Bay) (1899)
Fu-chou (1861)
Ting-chou
Hsing-hua
Lung-yen
Chien-ning
Hsia-mên, Amoy (1862)
Chang-chou
P'êng-hu, Hokoto, Pescadores Is.
T'ai-pei
T'ai-wan
T'ai-wan, Formosa (to Japan 1895)
T'ai-nan
An-p'ing
Eastern Sea
Shan-t'ou, Swatow (1860)
Chao-chou
Kuang-tung, Canton (1859)
San-shui
Kao-lung, Kaulun (1897)
Hsiang-chiang, Hongkong (1841 to England)
Macao (Portug.)
Southern Sea
115°
120°
125°

DEUTSCHE BANK IN CHINA

DEUTSCHE BANK IN CHINA

Piper
Munich Zurich

Contents

Foreword

Deutsche Bank can look back on a long and eventful history in China. The bank opened its first office in 1872, just two years after being founded in Berlin. When it set up a branch in China – the first outside Germany – it was simply fulfilling its mission "to facilitate commercial relations between Germany and overseas markets," as stated in the company's charter. Other reasons for the expansion were the spirit of enterprise and a Management Board member's knowledge of the country. Significant losses in the silver trade, however, led to this first foray into China being abandoned after three years.

Deutsch-Asiatische Bank, founded in Shanghai in 1889, was Deutsche Bank's second and far more successful attempt to penetrate the Chinese market. Its main activity was trade finance, but it soon began floating Chinese government bonds and financing railway and mining projects. In 1906, Deutsch-Asiatische Bank also started to issue its own banknotes in China.

The First World War ended Deutsche Bank's business activities in China for a second time. Deutsch-Asiatische Bank reopened some of its former branches several years after the war, but in 1945 all of them were closed again. The fourth new beginning on Chinese soil came with the opening of the Hong Kong branch in 1958. In 1972, the bank was folded into the new European Asian Bank, which was fully integrated into the Deutsche Bank Group in 1986. Since 1976, Deutsche Bank has operated its own offices in China: the first one in Hong Kong was followed by Beijing in 1981, Guangzhou in 1994 and Shanghai in 1995.

In recent years, Deutsche Bank's presence in China has taken on a new dimension. Organic growth and strategic investments have given the bank an outstanding position in investment banking, retail banking and asset management. Today, it already has more than 2,000 employees in China, including Hong Kong, and the number is growing rapidly.

Published in commemoration of the 50th anniversary of the reopening of the Hong Kong branch, this illustrated history tells an impressive story of our involvement in China over more than 136 years. At the same time, it encourages us to further increase our commitment to this great nation and its financial community.

Frankfurt am Main, August 2008 Josef Ackermann

Deutsche Bank in China 1872–2008 – An Overview

1.

The descriptions of China and Asia by Marco Polo, the Venetian traveller, are featured in some of the oldest books printed in Germany, dating back to 1477. Accounts of his travels had been circulating around Europe even much earlier. In the Middle Ages, the East was thought to be immensely rich in precious metals, spices and other goods coveted by the West, such as gold and silver, pepper and silk. Indeed, China and, to a lesser extent, Japan were the ultimate in adventure and opportunity, but they were also far away and inaccessible. Even the violent incursion into China and Japan in the middle of the 19th century did not turn these countries into European-dominated territories. This may explain why China remained so attractive to European travellers, especially businessmen, who believed that China was a world of unlimited opportunity. Sir Henry Pottinger, author of the Nanking Treaty, under which China was forced to open treaty ports in 1843 following the country's defeat in the Opium War, boasted to Manchester industrialists that he had given them access to a new world so gigantic that "all of the textile factories of Lancashire are not enough to supply even just one of its provinces with socks." Almost a hundred years later, a British ambassador still believed that the British economy could be restored to health if a handkerchief could be sold to each person in China.

Deutsche Bank's early involvement in Asia, especially China, is therefore quite natural in light of all the business prospects in the region. This book tells the story of this involvement. Deutsche's first advance into China was short-lived. The second, by Deutsch-Asiatische Bank (DAB) in 1889, was highly successful at first. Before the First

World War, DAB's main priority was to catch up with the much larger Hongkong and Shanghai Banking Corporation (HSBC). By the end of the war, however, most of the bank's overseas branches, real estate and assets had been lost. Unstable conditions in China between the two world wars made normal business operations nearly impossible, with the Second World War putting an end to them entirely. The latest return to mainland China in the 1980s was a consequence of Deng Xiaoping's reforms in the People's Republic. These reforms heralded the beginning of a new chapter that is still being written today. By the end of the 1990s, the bank was able to resume regular business and has been building on its former presence ever since to become part of the country's rapidly expanding financial and capital markets.

2.

In the 19th century, the world became much smaller and the distance between China and Europe much shorter, thanks to ocean cables, the opening of the Suez Canal and steamboats that dramatically reduced communication and travel times – all of which intensified trade. At the beginning of the 19th century, ships of the East India Company still required about six months to complete their journeys. Tea clippers, introduced later in the century, cut that time to as little as 90 days. Travel time was reduced still further with the opening of the Suez Canal in 1869, which shortened the route by 6,500 kilometres: new steamships now needed less than 65 days for the journey from the North Sea to Hong Kong. Passenger transportation benefitted from the shorter routes and faster ships. When Franz Urbig, at that time senior executive at Disconto-Gesellschaft, travelled to Shanghai in 1894 on behalf of Deutsch-Asiatische Bank, he left Berlin by train for Naples on November 19. There, he embarked on the Lloyd steamer "Gera" on November 28 and arrived in Shanghai on December 28.

The changes were even more dramatic in long-distance communications. The first deep-sea cable from England reached Alexandria in 1868, Bombay (now Mumbai) in

1870, Hong Kong in 1871, Yokohama in 1872 and Shanghai in 1873. The improvement in shipping links also gradually reduced the mailing time for a letter from London to Canton (Guangzhou) or Hong Kong: four to six months before 1835, two to three months by about 1840, 55 days in 1845 and as few as 43 days in 1860. The telegraph cut this time to just a few hours. As a result, China became more integrated into international trade, and the advantages previously enjoyed by the big trading houses with their better connections and the ability to store large quantities of goods started to dwindle. More and more merchants entered the Chinese market.

3.

Relative isolation was the normal state of affairs until the mid-19th century. Trade between China and the East India Company had intensified since the 18th century, with silk and tea being exchanged for silver. The Company's chronic trade deficit led to the rapid rise of opium, which, after cultivation in British India, was exported to China for consumption there. This stream of revenue from the British colony helped not only the East India Company improve its balance sheet but also Britain manage its public finances. The attempt by Chinese regional governors to stop the opium trade because of the drug's devastating effects on humans and productivity led to the Opium War in 1840 and, in its wake, to the forced opening of Chinese ports to Western merchants. Under the Treaty of Nanking, which ended the war, Hong Kong had to be leased to the British. Five ports opened to foreign trade: Canton (Guangzhou), Amoy (Xiamen), Foochowfoo (Fouzhou), Ningpo (Ningbo) and Shanghai. Rules on preferred status were relaxed, foreign merchants gained extraterritorial status, and gunboats were stationed in the ports to protect the merchants. This one-sided treaty, pushed through by the British under the same "open-door policy" that the Americans and French also imposed one year later, attracted merchants from all over the world to Shanghai in particular. The city grew to become China's main business hub, thanks to its location at the mouth of the Yangtze River and to the economically advanced region around it.

At the beginning of the 1860s, a Prussian delegation came to China with four warships and returned home with a trade agreement that conferred most-preferred and extraterritorial status on Prussian merchants, a regulation later transferred to the new German Empire in 1871. From this point on, Chinese exports also became more diverse. No longer were silk and tea the main exports, which faced growing Japanese and South Asian competition; raw cotton, beans, vegetable oils and various manufactured and agricultural products were also in demand. At the same time, imports grew, with Western goods playing an increasingly important role.

4.

At the beginning of the 1890s, nearly 30 German companies were operating in China. Many of them, especially the smaller ones, depended on European banks for trade finance for lack of a Chinese banking system. The British companies that succeeded the East India Company and that had prospered from the opium trade did not require financial assistance on a large scale. Established in 1865, HSBC leveraged its access to favourable funding at the world's largest and most productive financial centre, London, to offer its clients good terms and conditions for financing their trade activities. As trade with China was conducted almost completely in sterling to keep the exchange rate risk in China's silver-backed currency as low as possible, HSBC enjoyed a near unassailable position as far as a non-British bank was concerned. But there were international competitors, such as the French Comptoir d'Escompte, which had branches in East Asia from the early 1860s and, in the eyes of Deutsche Bank's founders, had been doing excellent business in the region. Business with China appeared particularly attractive to the newly established Deutsche Bank, which opened its doors in 1870 in Berlin with a focus on foreign trade finance. Its founding memorandum published the year before described Asia as an "important" region. In 1872, the bank seized the opportunity to enter the market. Deutsche Bank's Administrative Board convinced Hermann Wallich, the former head of the Shanghai branch of Comptoir d'Escompte, to join its

Management Board. Wallich then approached other members of the French bank to comment on Deutsche Bank's expansion plans. In response to Wallich's inquiry, J. Mammelsdorf, head of the Yokohama branch of Comptoir d'Escompte, expressed his views on fundamental policy issues: "Looking to the future as well as considering Germany's present commercial position, I believe that the time has come to bring German capital into international trade in order to politically strengthen and unify Germany. The imminent introduction of a uniform gold standard also makes it the duty of German institutions to enter the world stage." The war indemnities, which the French had to pay, would also reduce the German discount rate to such an extent that competition with the United Kingdom would become possible. Mammelsdorf also expected Asia's interest in a strengthened Germany to grow, speculating that silver exports from the country could give its own financial institutions in the region "an opportunity to establish extensive business operations and gain influential status."

Deutsche Bank's Management Board did not take Mammelsdorf's advice to open branches simultaneously in Hong Kong, Shanghai and Yokohama. Following a capital increase in 1872, the bank opened its first branch in Hamburg, and then in Shanghai and Yokohama a few months later. Hong Kong was left out because Georg von Siemens and Hermann Wallich, both members of the Management Board, considered its future to be less promising than Shanghai's. From then on, the German Emperor's navy travelled with letters of credit from Deutsche Bank and no longer used English banking services.

Demand for the bank's services was sluggish, however. The stock exchange crisis of 1873 and the subsequent economic downturn in Germany led to a sharp decline in business. Since China had no capital market and no possibility of establishing an adequate deposits business, the new branch in Shanghai needed its own silver-backed capital base to match the Chinese currency. Unfortunately, the capital assigned to the branch depreciated dramatically compared with the gold-backed pound sterling and the other gold currencies during the following years. The sale of silver by the German Empire and Deutsche Bank in connection with the introduction of the gold standard accelerated this devaluation process.

The collapse of day-to-day business and the large currency losses led to the closure of the Asian branches in 1875. Shanghai folded first with losses of 245,000 Marks, followed by Yokohama with 191,000 Marks. Combined, the Asian branches lost 10 per cent of their original capital. Consequently, Deutsche Bank had to downscale its ambitious goals. "We want to expressly emphasize that we are not abandoning our programme of supporting German overseas trade but will, in fact, continue to support it with the aid of our London branch, which is performing splendidly," the bank stated in its Annual Report for 1875. The growing use of the Mark as an international currency in China stopped, and efforts to introduce the German currency into other overseas markets were abandoned for the time being. From Germany's perspective, East Asian markets faced numerous unresolved problems. The currency risk, for instance, was extremely high, particularly in China; settlement in sterling therefore predominated. Consequently, foreign trade financing in the British currency through London banks, especially HSBC, which was well represented in London and China, was viewed not only as the safest solution, but often as the least expensive one as well. Before 1914, German merchants were on HSBC's Supervisory Board. Some reports in the London press even suggested that HSBC represented German interests.

Under these generally unfavourable conditions DAB was founded in 1889. It was jointly owned by the big German banks. Although Disconto-Gesellschaft played a leading role, Deutsche Bank also had a strong influence in decision-making. When the two banks merged in 1929, Deutsche Bank's weight increased and the history of DAB became part of Deutsche Bank's. The other members of the founding consortium were Bleichroeder, Berlin, Berliner Handels-Gesellschaft, Bank für Handel und Industrie (Darmstädter Bank), Rob. Warschauer & Co., Berlin, Mendelssohn & Co., Berlin, Jacob S.H. Stern, Frankfurt, M.A. v. Rothschild & Söhne in Frankfurt, Norddeutsche Bank in Hamburg, Sal. Oppenheim, Cologne, and Bayerische Hypotheken- und Wechsel-Bank in Munich. A symbolic share was held by the Seehandlung, later renamed the Prussian State Bank, reflecting the German government's backing for the new institution. The President of the Supervisory Board had to be confirmed by the German Emperor, reflecting the state's role. Without support from the Emperor and Chancellor Bismarck, the bank's founding would have been much more difficult.

The establishment of DAB was preceded by years of bickering among founding members over the type of bank they wanted and their respective influence in it. The Berlin government considered founding an "Imperial Bank" to finance German trade and provide credit to German banks abroad. The private banks strongly opposed a state solution and set up numerous overseas banks that competed with each other.

The experience of German banks in Chinese business was not particularly encouraging as the closure of Deutsche Bank's branch in Shanghai after only three years demonstrated. In 1883, Wallich sought to penetrate the Chinese bond market through the large English-Chinese trading company Jardine, Matheson & Co., but did not succeed. Adolph von Hansemann, the head of Disconto-Gesellschaft, tried to enter into business with Chinese railway bonds, but failed to beat the English competition, which did not allow German banks to operate on an equal footing in their field of activity. Von Hansemann reacted strongly and wrote to the Department of Foreign Affairs in Berlin: "Our experience again this time was that England recognizes as equals only those who display the serious will and strength to fight for such equality."

German industry was eager to do business with China. Friedrich Kleinwächter, who later became known for his research into cartels, drafted a Chinese railway law that was submitted to the Chinese government with the articles of association for a Chinese-German railway construction company – without success. The Chinese central government under Empress Dowager Cixi (Tzu Hsi) was not interested in railways. Nevertheless, in the summer of 1885, a delegation was sent to China "to study the commercial, financial and technical aspects of railway construction in China, with regard to issuing bonds, supplying railway materials and acquiring railway facilities, and to obtain the information and establish the contacts required initially to facilitate the achievement of these objectives." The four members of the delegation were Curt Erich, the authorized representative of Disconto-Gesellschaft, A.H. Exner of Deutsche Bank, Mr. Bethge, a government building official, and retired Lieutenant-Colonel Wagner of the Corps of Engineers. They returned in 1886 convinced that German companies would have little prospect of making headway in the bond and railway businesses in China if they did not have their own bank. Exner, Deutsche Bank's representative, even wrote a book in which he described the founding of a German-Asian bank as an urgent matter. Max von Brandt, the German envoy to China at the time, agreed entirely and stated that "if the amount of work and capital needed for lasting success in China appears to German industry and banks to be too great, then all of the efforts made by others will also remain futile due to their semi-platonic infatuation with the Chinese market."

He also repeatedly urged the founding of a bank in China, pointing out that English banks had to be used to finance exports, as the Chinese side was not in a position to pay immediately. German exports were therefore dependent on English goodwill. "To believe that English capitalists will support German industry in the long term in selling their manufactured goods on Chinese markets would be to underestimate their interest in their own patriotic industry in its struggle against foreign competitors," wrote von Brandt. "Once the representation of large German industries is transferred entirely to English hands, the disadvantages of such a position will become tangible, and much greater efforts and sacrifices will then have to be made to rectify the mistake that can now still be easily avoided."

Political pressure to set up a bank in Asia grew so strong that a syndicate was finally formed under Adolph von Hansemann's leadership. The big competitors, Disconto-Gesellschaft and Deutsche Bank, agreed to jointly establishing a German-Asian bank. Resistance came from a group centred on private bank Rob. Warschauer and Berliner Handels-Gesellschaft, which had successfully floated a mini-bond in China in 1887. State intervention finally led to a compromise. After long negotiations, the consortium's representatives finally met on New Year's Eve in 1887 to clarify the respective stakes and the role of the Seehandlung (Prussian State Bank), which was reluctant to become a shareholder. Massive political pressure had to be applied before the Seehandlung finally agreed to a full commitment. Herbert von Bismarck, the son of Chancellor Otto von Bismarck, wrote on January 9, 1889, to Prussian Minister of Finance Adolf von Scholz: "It still appears urgently advisable that the Seehandlung should participate in order to balance out personal rivalries in the competing groups of banks through the weight of its authoritative position; apart from this aspect, however, the bankers involved place special emphasis on the fact that our company can only succeed against the strong competition from English banks in China if part of the bill business between China and Germany is routed through an institution of such high repute as the Seehandlung."

Without the political will of the Chancellery in Berlin, the fierce competition between the banks would probably have scuppered the bank's founding, which finally took place on February 12, 1889. Its share capital of 20 million Marks in silver was anything but attractive, however. The value of the investment was likely to depreciate rapidly with the price of silver. The new bank was founded in accordance with German stock corporation law, but its capital denominated in Chinese silver taels (5,000 shares of

1,000 taels each). Max von Schinckel, a member of the Management Board of Norddeutsche Bank at the time, wrote in his memoirs published at the end of the 1920s: "At Bismarck's urging and after much back and forth in Berlin, Deutsch-Asiatische Bank was finally established. As no one was keen on the risk that would be entailed by contributing capital in silver taels, the bank was ultimately formed by an extensive group of all the banks and bankers of repute in Germany. There were fears right from the start that so many cooks would spoil the Asian broth. Over the years, however, the zeal subsided into activity, and management soon passed into the expert hands of [Supervisory Board] Chairman Franz Urbig, proprietor of Disconto-Gesellschaft."

DAB was founded on the premises of Disconto-Gesellschaft in Berlin. The first members of the Management Board were Curt Erich, Director of Disconto-Gesellschaft, and Erich Breustedt, authorized representative at Deutsche Bank. Shanghai became the bank's principal place of business. Ferdinand Rinkel, authorized representative at Disconto-Gesellschaft, took over the management and formation of the Shanghai office. With the necessary credit commitments from London-based Rothschild and Seehandlung in his luggage, he embarked for Shanghai in September 1889 with Mr. Kalb, a former employee of Reiss & Co. with business experience in China. DAB's Supervisory Board had 14 members. Its first Chairman was Hans Rüdorff, a former senior Treasury official and at that time President of Preussische Central-Boden-Kredit AG. After his death, he was succeeded as Chairman by Adolph Frentzel, President of the "Elders of the Berlin Mercantile Community." Both men were confirmed in this position by the German Emperor. In accordance with the articles of association, the official location of the Supervisory Board was Berlin, where at least five members of the Supervisory Board also had to reside. Three-quarters had to live in Germany, and all of them in Europe to keep DAB under tight management control from Berlin.

5.

Day-to-day business was off to a bad start. The majority of German merchants in China remained with HSBC. Given the continuing fall in the price of silver, many believed that doing business with DAB was risky. Kalb reported on the difficulties in establishing closer business contacts with German companies in China, even though they were offered favourable terms and conditions, and despite occasional appeals to their patriotism. The bank achieved some success with larger companies, but the smaller ones stayed with HSBC, which, anticipating competition, had opened a branch in Hamburg in 1889. To establish a solid day-to-day business took time, as direct cooperation with Chinese partners was not possible. Trading companies and banks had to depend on the services of "compradores." These were Chinese nationals who worked in foreign companies, supervised Chinese staff, maintained business contacts with China and served as interpreters. Members of DAB's Supervisory Board in Berlin also caused problems. They were keen to keep the business activities of their Chinese branches under tight control. Complaints from local bank employees about a lack of leeway were ignored. As Franz Urbig summarized it: Risky business requires strict control. The competition at HSBC, though, was quick to point out that DAB enjoyed little independence and that decisions were made in Berlin without knowledge of Chinese conditions. German bankers, for instance, approved loans, which ran counter to Chinese custom and practice. A further negative factor was the sharp fall in the price of silver, which dropped 40 per cent between 1891 and 1895. This reduced the value of the paid-up capital accordingly, and at the same time strongly curtailed Chinese imports.

So business sputtered along, eventually costing Ferdinand Rinkel his job. He was succeeded by Ferdinand Rehders and finally by Franz Urbig. Initially, Urbig took over the branch in Tientsin (now Tianjin), close to Peking (now Beijing), the centre of power in China. He had a talent for languages and consequently established good contacts in Peking.

As a consequence of its defeat in the war against Japan, which ended with the Treaty of Shimonoseki, China had to pay reparations of 48 million pounds. This was an enormous sum, equivalent to roughly 900 million Marks. To pay Japan Peking had to secure a loan on the international financial markets. News that the first tranche, valued at 16 million pounds, had been placed by a Russian bank at favourable terms and conditions on the French capital market upset HSBC, which had previously played a leading role in the Chinese bond business. Given the disinterest of London investors in Chinese securities and the uncertainty over whether the stated amounts could be placed in London, the English bank struck an agreement with DAB for both banks to participate in the Chinese bond issuing business on an equal footing.

Franz Urbig and HSBC's representative in Peking worked out the bond conditions and prepared them for signature. After tough negotiations, the banks signed the preliminary agreement in March 1896; the final Imperial edict on a 5 per cent bond for 16 million pounds was issued on March 24, 1896. Its success was confirmed by the 50-fold oversubscription of the German portion. In later bond issues, DAB and/or the related syndicate for Asian transactions also subscribed large amounts from the HSBC portions, resulting in the German capital market becoming a pillar of support for the joint bond operations. This development was a breakthrough for DAB. From now on the bank participated in all other major Chinese bond issues. Cooperation with HSBC went smoothly. Franz Urbig later regretted that such German-English cooperation did not extend to other fields. "The position of Deutsch-Asiatische Bank was considerably advanced by this politically important success," he wrote. "The bank was now seen as representing a capital strength that had been underestimated until then, particularly in England, and with which much could have been achieved in the course of time if people in Germany had not overlooked the value of political friendship with England so early on."

After the revolution of 1911 and the end of Imperial China, DAB was instrumental in the stabilization of the new republican government and played a leading role in the successful completion of the so-called "reorganization bond," despite Russian and Japanese efforts to obstruct it. The bank made a good profit on the bonds, whereas China in most cases did not.

As repayment for China's debt of gratitude to Germany, which had prevented the cession of the Liaodong peninsula, the German Empire felt entitled to occupy the Bay of Kiautchou (Jiaozhou) with the port town of Tsing-Tao (now Qingdao), and to lease it from China for 99 years as a base for the Emperor's navy. As a consequence, DAB became a kind of state bank of Kiautchou with its own banknotes, its own mortgage department and comprehensive financing functions for the German colony and the Imperial German navy. These new activities, however, generated only modest earnings. By contrast, bonds and concessions – especially railway concessions – promised substantial profits. Due to the continued weakening of the Chinese government after 1895, its resistance to issuing railway concessions could ultimately be overcome. Strong interest groups emerged seeking to obtain concessions, set up railway construction and operating companies and to finance them. Starting in 1898 in Berlin, Adolph von Hansemann persistently urged that action be taken on the mining and railway issue, considering that the Bay of Kiautchou Lease Agreement entitled Germany to railway and mining concessions in Shantung (now Shandong) Province. On June 1, 1889, these concessions were formally granted. The Shantung Mining Company was founded in October 1899. Von Hansemann chaired the Supervisory Board of the company with a capital of 12 million Marks. Led by DAB, the Shantung Railway Company was founded on June 14, 1899 with capital of 54 million Marks and again with von Hansemann as Supervisory Board Chairman. The railway project proved successful compared to the mining company, a loss-making business that was finally taken over by the railway company. Despite problems with building the railway and difficulties in procuring materials from

Germany, on some sections railway operations began in 1901. The railway company paid dividends that rose gradually from 4 per cent to a peak at 7.5 per cent in 1913.

The relatively small concessions in Shantung Province were not enough for DAB, however. The bank saw possibilities to achieve larger profits with railways in the Yangtse area between Shanghai and Hankow (now Hankou, part of Wuhan) and with links between the north and Shanghai, such as the Tientsin-Pukow route. Unfortunately, DAB was unable to win over HSBC to its idea. The English partner kept to the agreement on a common bond policy, but declined to enter into other common projects. In fact, the English worked to keep the Germans away from the Yangtse, which they regarded as their own sphere of interest. Joint railway projects were therefore not realized.

DAB's day-to-day business improved gradually, but remained subject to strong fluctuations due to the volatility of the silver price, the intransparent currency situation, unstable political conditions and frequent natural disasters in China. All in all, though, in 1913 the bank could look back on a successful period of growth: In Germany, in addition to Hamburg it had a branch in Berlin, opened in 1896 to place bonds on the German market. Its presence in Asia was broad. Besides numerous branches in China, it maintained offices in Japan, Calcutta (India) and Singapore.

The bank had established a strong position on the bond market; foreign exchange business was expanding. Franz Urbig described the "healthy development" of the bank, which had freed itself from the political bond market, to the Director of the Shanghai office as follows: "You must always assume that I attach greater importance to current business than to everything else, because I consider it to be the source of our regular profits. I regard arbitrage as a useful activity and at the same time as the best basis for training managers and personnel. But syndicate business should only serve to improve our external position and at the same time our dividend."

The bank held back from acquiring industrial shareholdings for the simple reason that it could not operate the companies itself: an unwritten Chinese law allowed no effective control of local companies by foreign businesses. As Franz Urbig told the General Meeting: "There is no justification for the statements repeatedly made in public that our bank and the financial circles related to it show excessive restraint towards Chinese industrial companies. Proposals have occasionally reached us concerning loans with a long and unpredictable maturity for the purpose of founding, expanding or continuing such companies. All these enterprises, whose activities include coal and iron ore mining, the construction of private railways, the production of cement, sugar, etc., are purely under Chinese management ... Since China has no codified law, the lender's rights at such a company are unclear. Even less clear, however, are the duties of the persons performing the management function. Experience in the history of private Chinese companies with such legal conditions cannot be described as encouraging to European lenders. To offer shares or bonds of such purely Chinese companies would be incompatible not only with the principles of the German stock exchange listing authorities, but also with the standing of highly reputed banks." Since the Chinese refused to set up their companies in accordance with German law, and since the option of having purely German management personnel in Chinese companies was seen as too risky, the bank decided against financing locally owned businesses.

This restraint did not hurt business, but actually protected it, or so people thought in light of French losses. At any rate, profits were satisfactory. The largest share of profit was generated in Shanghai, followed by Tsing-Tao, Hong Kong, Tientsin and Tsinanfu, which had previously incurred losses. The situation in Peking was stable, thanks largely to good government contacts. The local branch continuously generated good profits. DAB was in good shape after 26 years of expansion; net profit had been high and rising since the turn of the century, with a short interruption during the revolutionary period; the dividend had been 6 to 10 per cent and fluctuated between 125 and 275 Marks per share (par value 1,000 Marks); and the principal source of profit before the outbreak of the First World War was foreign currency business.

6.

The war destroyed all this in a matter of weeks. Before 1914 German bankers supported the German Empire and its great power politics. They regarded the success of the Empire and of their banks as mutually supportive. But it was clear to everyone that a major war would be fatal for the banking business. And so it was: the war spelled the end of DAB. Trade between Germany and China ceased. Kiautchou was conquered by the Japanese, the branch there was shut down. The branches in the British sphere of interest were closed as well, their employees detained and their assets liquidated and later credited to the reparation account. The new branch premises in Hong Kong, completed in spring 1914 at a cost of 326,278 Hong Kong silver dollars, were auctioned off in the following year, despite protests from the German Department of Foreign Affairs.

Heinrich Cordes, Manager of the Peking branch, ventured into politics on his own by trying in 1916 to arouse the interest of warlord Yuan Shikai, who had seized power in China, in a German bond issue in order to keep him from entering the war on the side of the Allied powers. The bond issue failed, however. Bowing to international pressure, China declared war on the German Empire in 1917 and seized DAB's branches and their assets. The buildings were sold, their assets confiscated, all concessions withdrawn and the debt service on the various bonds was stopped. After the ceasefire in 1918, most Germans had to leave China within two days, taking with them a maximum of 150 pounds of luggage. Only a few DAB employees stayed in the country.

In the summer of 1919, China declared an end to the war, but did not sign the Treaty of Versailles. Long negotiations on German assets in China – totalling more than one billion gold Marks before 1914 – followed, which finally led to an agreement in 1921 in which Germany waived its rights under the Treaty of Kiautchou and declared its readiness to pay reparations. China was to receive half of the German assets, stopping the liquidation process in return and giving back the rest. De facto only a small part of the private assets was returned. DAB was exempted from this, however, since it was considered public property. The bank tried to retrieve its books and, in particular, sought to keep at least the buildings that had not yet been sold and to obtain the resumption of debt service on bonds – all to no avail. The bank therefore turned to the German government for compensation and finally received 3.5 million silver dollars, which it used as working capital to restart operations in China.

Franz Urbig was sceptical. He was inclined to give up the bank, but in the end the bank's representatives in China managed to change his mind. At the end of 1922, the Supervisory Board voted to re-open the branches. The bank's representatives first worked as agents of the Hamburg branch in Shanghai, Canton and Tientsin in rented offices, and in Hankow and Peking in the old buildings owned by the bank. It was not until 1924 that the bank's books were returned, as were its buildings in Peking and Hankow, and it was re-mandated to service a railway bond. An agreement with Germany gave the bank a total of 6 million silver dollars, minus the payments already made. Bank accounts were re-established in 1927. Between 1914 and 1926 the value of assets decreased by 4 million Shanghai taels; the bank's capital was reduced accordingly.

In 1920, the number of German firms in China had dwindled to nine. By 1927, it had increased again to 307. Germany's share in China's trade grew considerably. But due to its own funding difficulties, DAB was unable to settle many transactions. HSBC and other banks were stronger than ever. Chiang Kai-shek's (Jiang Jieshi) rise to power offered hope for an end to the chaos in China and for previous bond rights to be restored. "Consolidation, if it comes at all in the foreseeable future, will mean unification of the country, centralized power, financial reform, codified law," Urbig wrote to Shanghai on August 21, 1928. "Only on that basis can there be the security to make the old bonds valuable again and new ones possible." Under these conditions, new bonds could be considered, but, despite negotiations, none were realized, as the Chinese Nationalist government wanted to rid itself of the one-sided agreements.

The following years were characterized by continuous turmoil. During the Great Depression, trade collapsed and China became engaged in a civil war. Under these circumstances, DAB was unwilling and unable to grant any new loans. After closing each of the years between 1927 and 1930 with a profit, between 1931 and 1934 the bank posted losses. In fact, a request had to be made to the envoy in Peking for an advance of 100,000 pounds, only to be followed by criticism from the German Consul in Tsing-Tao that German merchants in China were dissatisfied with DAB's high costs and poor services. The consolidation of the Chinese Nationalist government finally led to a currency reform, which introduced a national currency decoupled from silver. Investments in infrastructure stimulated business from 1934 to 1937. Profits were made again, as Germany emerged as China's most important trade partner.

The Second Sino-Japanese War (War to Resist the Japanese), once again brought business activity to a partial standstill. It revived, but only to a limited extent, after the Japanese had completed their occupation of large parts of central and southern China. The outbreak of the Second World War initially brought an upswing in business activity, with exports of goods continuing through the Soviet Union. But when the Soviet Union and the US entered the war in 1941, the situation changed dramatically.

The end of the war in Asia also spelled the end of DAB's operations. In the summer of 1945, its branches were taken over by employees of the Bank of China. The German employees continued their work, though, until the following year when they were finally forced to stop under humiliating conditions, detained and repatriated to Germany in the summer of 1946.

7.

Little remained of DAB in Germany, either. The Berlin branch operations were terminated by the Russian occupation forces. What was left was a handful of employees and a building in Hamburg, out of which first European Asian Bank, then Deutsche Bank (Asia) and finally Deutsche Bank's Asian business developed. For years activities in mainland China were out of the question. Singapore and Hong Kong became the most important bases in Asia for the financing of German foreign trade with China, which quickly gained importance from the 1950s onwards. Behind the U.S., Germany grew to become the second most important Western trading partner of the new People's Republic of China.

The Communist government nationalized the financial sector along Soviet lines. Foreign institutions left the country; only HSBC retained a liaison office in Shanghai. After Mao's death in 1976, the country cautiously opened itself again to the West, supported by the belief that only intensive economic cooperation with industrialized nations would allow a rapid modernization of the Chinese economy. Hans-Otto Thierbach, a member of Deutsche Bank's Management Board, reported at the end of 1977 after a trip to China with a delegation headed by Foreign Minister Hans-Dietrich Genscher, that China intended to become a "major industrial power" by the year 2000. Thierbach was sceptical of the prospects, though. He did not consider China to be an attractive partner or country to do business for Deutsche Bank in the foreseeable future. He ruled out opening a branch in China but was in favour of setting up a representative office. This office opened in 1981 in Peking, with the task of supporting contacts between Deutsche Bank customers and Chinese organizations and authorities.

When Hermann Josef Abs, the grand old man of Deutsche Bank, visited China in 1984 at the invitation of China International Trust and Investment Corporation, his executive assistant reported on Shanghai, the country's business capital: "Unlike Beijing, Shanghai does not have a dense road network. We did not have the impression that Shanghai, with its more than 11 million inhabitants, was one of the biggest cities in the world. The relatively narrow streets are lined by shady trees, and most of the low, two- to three-floor buildings are still made of wood. At first sight, the city is hardly recognizable as the country's centre of light and heavy industry." In 1987 Deutsche Bank's representative in Beijing stated that "much time and much patience" were needed for doing business in China, but that it had been possible to "build up a very broad banking business with Chinese entities, especially with the country's foreign trade bank, the Bank of China." The focus was on the investment goods industry.

With the further opening of China, business contacts grew. A second Deutsche Bank representative office was opened in 1994 in Guangzhou (Canton), the main business centre in the south. One year later, it became Deutsche Bank's first branch office in the People's Republic. In nearby Hong Kong, a representative office had already been established in 1976, and upgraded to a branch office three years later. As China's economic growth and economic reforms rapidly gained momentum, far beyond what had been thought possible, the scope of business for foreign banks increased substantially, and in 1999 Deutsche Bank opened a second branch in mainland China in Shanghai. In November 2004 the representative office in Beijing received branch status. China's entry into the WTO in 2001 in particular opened up the Chinese financial market, step by step, to foreign institutions.

Deutsche Bank's activities in China continued to expand beyond trade finance and politically initiated business to include investment banking services like Chinese currency trading. With its dynamic economic growth, China also became increasingly attractive for asset management and private wealth management activities. Deutsche Bank gradually expanded its business by introducing tailored products and securing selective shareholdings in Chinese companies and joint ventures. Its shareholdings in the Chinese fund management company Harvest Fund and in the commercial Hua Xia Bank opened the doors to business with Chinese consumers. At the beginning of 2008, Deutsche Bank (China) Co., Ltd. was allowed to launch operations as a fully licensed Chinese subsidiary of Deutsche Bank AG with the right to conduct business in the local currency. The former branches of Deutsche Bank AG in Beijing, Shanghai and Guangzhou were converted into branches of Deutsche Bank (China), headquartered in Beijing. After more than 136 years, several false starts and countless setbacks, Deutsche Bank has found its rightful place as one of the leading foreign players in China with even greater prospects going forward.

BEGINNINGS IN CHINA
1872–1875

01

Geschäfts=Instruktion
für die
Agenturen der Deutschen Bank
in Ost-Asien.

§. 1.

Die Agenturen der Deutschen Bank in Ost=Asien werden die Firma „Deutsche Bank, Actien=Gesellschaft, Shanghai resp. Yokohama führen und dem Zweck des Haupt=Instituts entsprechend Bankgeschäfte aller Art betreiben, insbesondere die Handelsbeziehungen zwischen Ost=Asien und den Märkten anderer Länder fördern und erleichtern und die deutsche Valuta in diesen Ländern einzuführen versuchen.

§. 2.

Für die Geschäftsführung im Allgemeinen ist das unter dem 10. März 1870 Allerhöchst vollzogene Statut der Deutschen Bank maßgebend, insofern nicht solches in seinen einzelnen Theilen durch nachstehende specielle Bestimmungen ergänzt wird.

§. 3.

Die Grundbedingung aller einzugehenden Geschäfte ist angemessene Sicherheit für die Bank.

§. 4.

Die zum Geschäftsbetrieb nöthigen Geldmittel werden den Agenturen von der Direction überwiesen, solche sind zunächst auf 2,000,000 Thaler für Shanghai, 1,000,000 Thaler für Yokohama festgesetzt. Die Agenturen haben dabei volle Benutzung der bei ihnen hinterlegten Gelder. Eine Erhöhung oder Verringerung des Betriebscapitals unterliegt der Anordnung der Berliner Direction.

02

01 Hermann Wallich, member of Deutsche Bank's Management Board from 1870 to 1894, was the expert on China.

02 "Business Instructions for Deutsche Bank Agencies" in Shanghai and Yokohama.

03 This is where it all began. Deutsche Bank's Berlin headquarters (building to the right) in 1872.

03

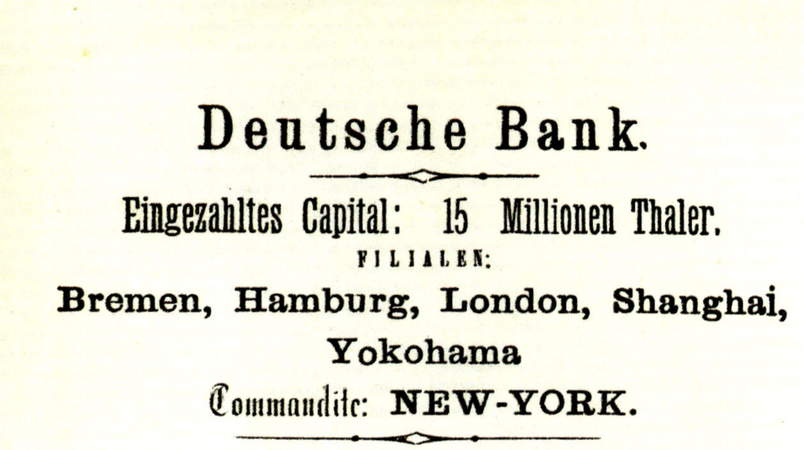

Deutsche Bank.

Eingezahltes Capital: 15 Millionen Thaler.

FILIALEN:

Bremen, Hamburg, London, Shanghai,

Yokohama

Commandite: NEW-YORK.

04

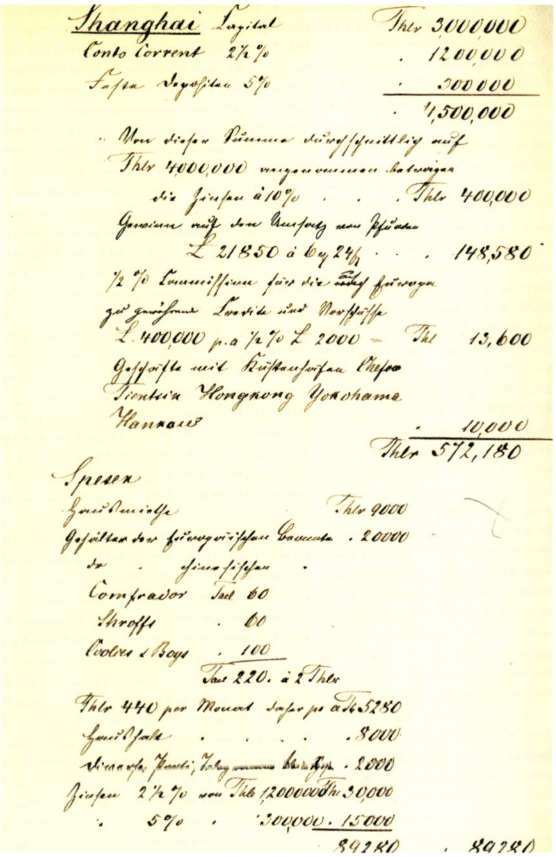

Shanghai Capital Thlr 3000000

Conto Corrent 2½ % . 1200000

Cassa Depositen 5 % . 300000

. 4,500,000

Thlr 4000000

Thlr 400,000

£ 21850 à 6 2⅔ . . . 148,580

£ 400,000 p.a ½ % £ 2000 – Thl 13,600

Tientsin Hongkong Yokohama

Hankow . 10,000

Thlr 572,180

Spesen

Thlr 9000

. 20000

Comprador Taels 60

Shroffs . 60

Coolies & Boys . 100

Taels 220. à 2 Thlr

Thlr 440 per Monat . 5280

. 8000

. 2000

2½ % Thlr 1200000 Thlr 30,000

5 % 300000 . 15000

89280 . 89280

05

04 Deutsche Bank's letterhead in 1873 with a list of its branches at the time.

05 Calculations for the Shanghai branch in 1873.

06 The port of Shanghai around 1860 with the Imperial Maritime Customs House in the background.

07 The Imperial Maritime Customs House in Shanghai around 1880.

06

07

08

09

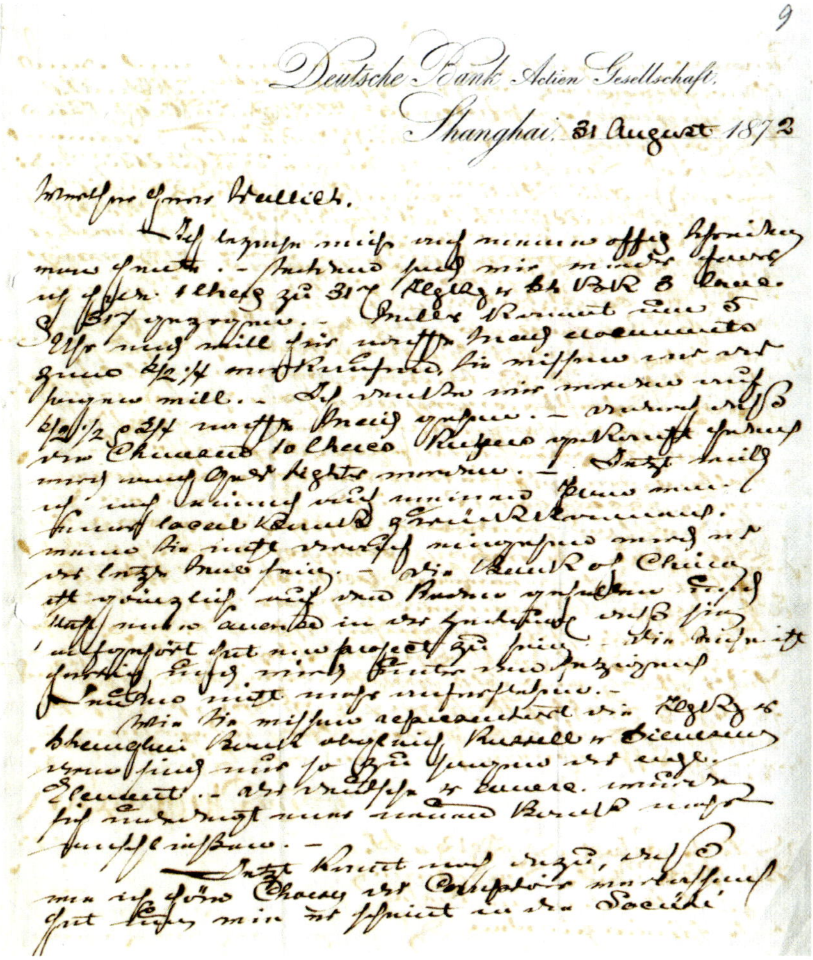
Deutsche Bank Actien Gesellschaft.
Shanghai, 31 August 1872

10

11

08 Shanghai street scene in the 1870s.

09 The German Consulate General in Shanghai around 1880.

10 Letter from Shanghai branch manager Emil Seligmann to Hermann Wallich in Berlin dated August 31, 1872.

11 A Shanghai compradore in 1874. Compradores were members of the Chinese merchant class who aided Western traders and businesses in China.

DEUTSCH-ASIATISCHE BANK
1889–1914

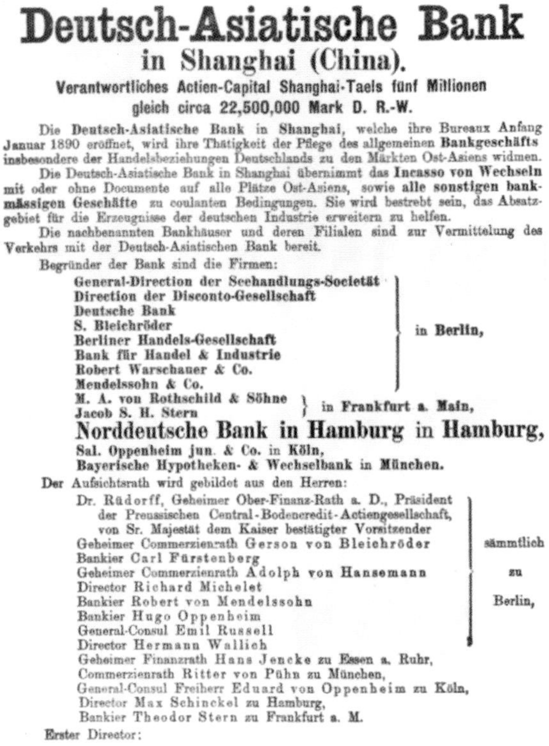

Deutsch-Asiatische Bank
in Shanghai (China).
Verantwortliches Actien-Capital Shanghai-Taels fünf Millionen gleich circa 22,500,000 Mark D. R.-W.

Die **Deutsch-Asiatische Bank** in **Shanghai**, welche ihre Bureaux Anfang **Januar** 1890 eröffnet, wird ihre Thätigkeit der Pflege des allgemeinen **Bankgeschäfts** insbesondere der Handelsbeziehungen Deutschlands zu den Märkten Ost-Asiens widmen.

Die Deutsch-Asiatische Bank in Shanghai übernimmt das **Incasso von Wechseln** mit oder ohne Documente auf alle Plätze Ost-Asiens, sowie **alle sonstigen bankmässigen Geschäfte** zu coulanten Bedingungen. Sie wird bestrebt sein, das Absatzgebiet für die Erzeugnisse der deutschen Industrie erweitern zu helfen.

Die nachbenannten Bankhäuser und deren Filialen sind zur Vermittelung des Verkehrs mit der Deutsch-Asiatischen Bank bereit.

Begründer der Bank sind die Firmen:

General-Direction der Seehandlungs-Societät
Direction der Disconto-Gesellschaft
Deutsche Bank
S. Bleichröder
Berliner Handels-Gesellschaft
Bank für Handel & Industrie
Robert Warschauer & Co.
Mendelssohn & Co.
} in **Berlin,**

M. A. von Rothschild & Söhne
Jacob S. H. Stern
} in **Frankfurt a. Main,**

Norddeutsche Bank in Hamburg in **Hamburg,**
Sal. Oppenheim jun. & Co. in **Köln,**
Bayerische Hypotheken- & Wechselbank in **München.**

Der Aufsichtsrath wird gebildet aus den Herren:

Dr. Rüdorff, Geheimer Ober-Finanz-Rath a. D., Präsident der Preussischen Central-Bodencredit-Actiengesellschaft, von Sr. Majestät dem Kaiser bestätigter Vorsitzender
Geheimer Commerzienrath Gerson von Bleichröder
Bankier Carl Fürstenberg
Geheimer Commerzienrath Adolph von Hansemann
Director Richard Michelet
Bankier Robert von Mendelssohn
Bankier Hugo Oppenheim
General-Consul Emil Russell
Director Hermann Wallich
} sämmtlich zu Berlin,

Geheimer Finanzrath Hans Jencke zu Essen a. Ruhr,
Commerzienrath Ritter von Pühn zu München,
General-Consul Freiherr Eduard von Oppenheim zu Köln,
Director Max Schinckel zu Hamburg,
Bankier Theodor Stern zu Frankfurt a. M.

Erster Director:

01

02

FOUNDATION IN BERLIN

01 Foundation announcement of Deutsch-Asiatische Bank from 1889 listing the syndicate of participating banks.

02 From 1864 to 1903, Adolph von Hansemann was in charge of Disconto-Gesellschaft and represented it on the Supervisory Board of Deutsch-Asiatische Bank.

03 Disconto-Gesellschaft headquarters in Berlin at the end of the 19th century. Disconto-Gesellschaft was the largest shareholder of Deutsch-Asiatische Bank. In 1929, it merged with Deutsche Bank.

04 Deutsche Bank was the second largest shareholder of Deutsch-Asiatische Bank, whose Berlin headquarters are shown here in 1895.

03

04

01

02

03

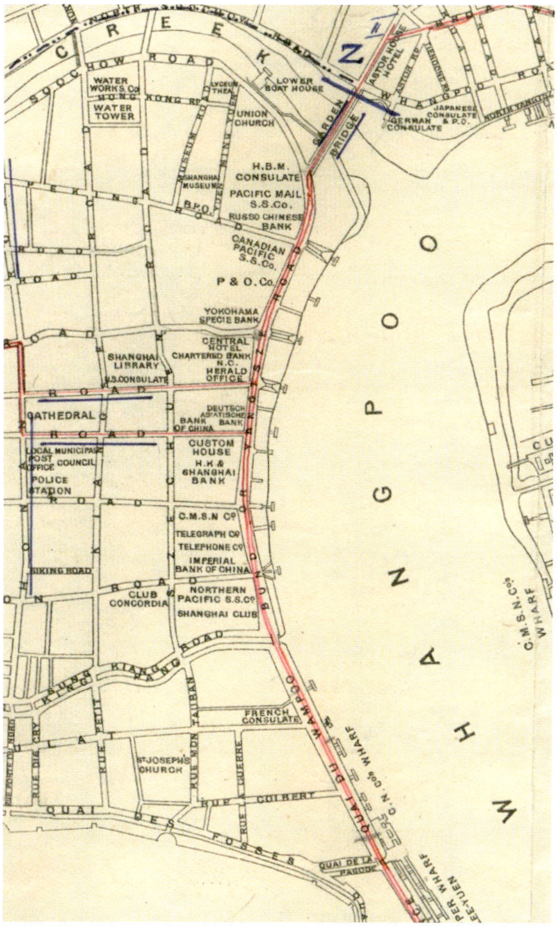

04

SHANGHAI

01 The port of Shanghai and the "Bund" around 1900.

02 The Customs House in Shanghai around 1905, with the Deutsch-Asiatische Bank building on the right.

03 Deutsch-Asiatische Bank on the "Bund" in Shanghai.

04 Map of Shanghai with the banking district along the "Bund" around 1900.

05

05 Share of Deutsch-Asiatische Bank with a nominal value of 1,000 Shanghai taels from 1906.

06 In 1898, Deutsch-Asiatische Bank participated in the issuance of the Chinese Imperial Government Loan amounting to 16 million pounds.

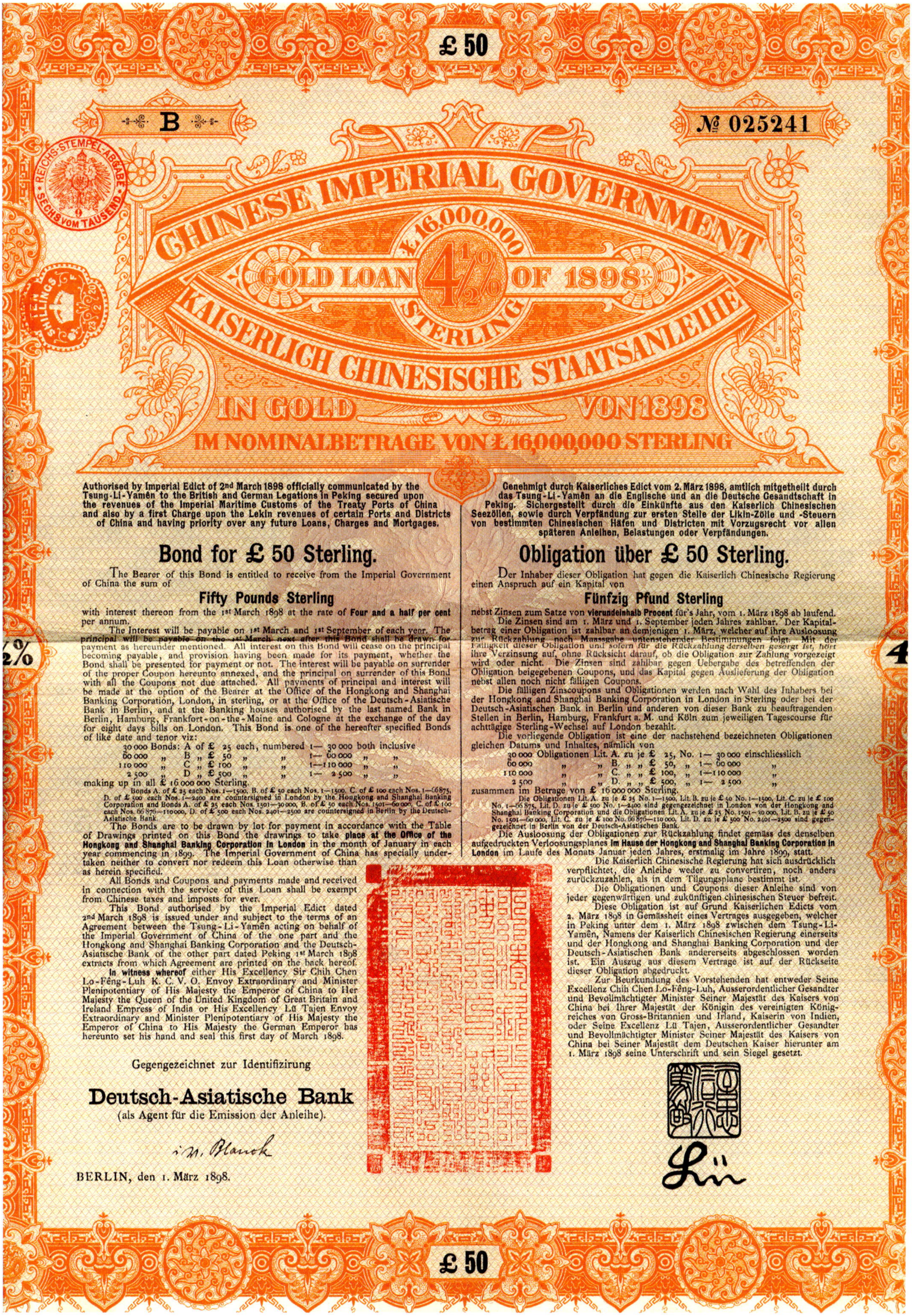
£ 50

B — № 025241

REICHS-STEMPEL-ABGABE SECHS VOM TAUSEND

CHINESE IMPERIAL GOVERNMENT

£ 16,000,000 GOLD LOAN 4½% OF 1898 STERLING

KAISERLICH CHINESISCHE STAATSANLEIHE

IN GOLD VON 1898

IM NOMINALBETRAGE VON £ 16,000,000 STERLING

Authorised by Imperial Edict of 2nd March 1898 officially communicated by the Tsung-Li-Yamên to the British and German Legations in Peking secured upon the revenues of the Imperial Maritime Customs of the Treaty Ports of China and also by a first Charge upon the Lekin revenues of certain Ports and Districts of China and having priority over any future Loans, Charges and Mortgages.

Bond for £ 50 Sterling.

The Bearer of this Bond is entitled to receive from the Imperial Government of China the sum of

Fifty Pounds Sterling

with interest thereon from the 1st March 1898 at the rate of **Four and a half per cent** per annum.

The Interest will be payable on 1st March and 1st September of each year. The principal will be payable on the 1st March next after this Bond shall be drawn for payment as hereunder mentioned. All interest on this Bond will cease on the principal becoming payable, and provision having been made for its payment, whether the Bond shall be presented for payment or not. The interest will be payable on surrender of the proper Coupon hereunto annexed, and the principal on surrender of this Bond with all the Coupons not due attached. All payments of principal and interest will be made at the option of the Bearer at the Office of the Hongkong and Shanghai Banking Corporation, London, in sterling, or at the Office of the Deutsch-Asiatische Bank in Berlin, and at the Banking houses authorised by the last named Bank in Berlin, Hamburg, Frankfort-on-the-Maine and Cologne at the exchange of the day for eight days bills on London. This Bond is one of the hereafter specified Bonds of like date and tenor viz:

30 000 Bonds:	A of £ 25	each,	numbered	1— 30 000	both inclusive
60 000 „	B „ £ 50	„	„	1— 60 000	„ „
110 000 „	C „ £ 100	„	„	1—110 000	„ „
2 500 „	D „ £ 500	„	„	1— 2 500	„ „

making up in all £ 16 000 000 Sterling.

Bonds A. of £ 25 each Nos. 1—1500, B. of £ 50 each Nos. 1—1500, C. of £ 100 each Nos. 1—66875, D. of £ 500 each Nos. 1—2400 are countersigned in London by the Hongkong and Shanghai Banking Corporation and Bonds A. of £ 25 each Nos. 1501—30000, B. of £ 50 each Nos. 1501—60000, C. of £ 100 each Nos. 66 876—110000, D. of £ 500 each Nos. 2401—2500 are countersigned in Berlin by the Deutsch-Asiatische Bank.

The Bonds are to be drawn by lot for payment in accordance with the Table of Drawings printed on this Bond the drawings to take **place at the Office of the Hongkong and Shanghai Banking Corporation in London** in the month of January in each year commencing in 1899. The Imperial Government of China has specially undertaken neither to convert nor redeem this Loan otherwise than as herein specified.

All Bonds and Coupons and payments made and received in connection with the service of this Loan shall be exempt from Chinese taxes and imposts for ever.

This Bond authorised by the Imperial Edict dated 2nd March 1898 is issued under and subject to the terms of an Agreement between the Tsung-Li-Yamên acting on behalf of the Imperial Government of China of the one part and the Hongkong and Shanghai Banking Corporation and the Deutsch-Asiatische Bank of the other part dated Peking 1st March 1898 extracts from which Agreement are printed on the back hereof.

In witness whereof either His Excellency Sir Chih Chen Lo-Fêng-Luh K. C. V. O. Envoy Extraordinary and Minister Plenipotentiary of His Majesty the Emperor of China to Her Majesty the Queen of the United Kingdom of Great Britain and Ireland Empress of India or His Excellency Lü Tajen Envoy Extraordinary and Minister Plenipotentiary of His Majesty the Emperor of China to His Majesty the German Emperor has hereunto set his hand and seal this first day of March 1898.

Gegengezeichnet zur Identifizirung

Deutsch-Asiatische Bank

(als Agent für die Emission der Anleihe).

BERLIN, den 1. März 1898.

Genehmigt durch Kaiserliches Edict vom 2. März 1898, amtlich mitgetheilt durch das Tsung-Li-Yamên an die Englische und an die Deutsche Gesandtschaft in Peking. Sichergestellt durch die Einkünfte aus den Kaiserlich Chinesischen Seezöllen, sowie durch Verpfändung zur ersten Stelle der Likin-Zölle und -Steuern von bestimmten Chinesischen Häfen und Districten mit Vorzugsrecht vor allen späteren Anleihen, Belastungen oder Verpfändungen.

Obligation über £ 50 Sterling.

Der Inhaber dieser Obligation hat gegen die Kaiserlich Chinesische Regierung einen Anspruch auf ein Kapital von

Fünfzig Pfund Sterling

nebst Zinsen zum Satze von **vierundeinhalb Procent** für's Jahr, vom 1. März 1898 ab laufend.

Die Zinsen sind am 1. März und 1. September jeden Jahres zahlbar. Der Kapitalbetrag einer Obligation ist zahlbar an demjenigen 1. März, welcher auf ihre Ausloosung zur Rückzahlung nach Maassgabe untenstehender Bestimmungen folgt. Mit der Fälligkeit dieser Obligation und sofern für die Rückzahlung derselben gesorgt ist, hört ihre Verzinsung auf, ohne Rücksicht darauf, ob die Obligation zur Zahlung vorgezeigt wird oder nicht. Die Zinsen sind zahlbar gegen Uebergabe des betreffenden der Obligation beigegebenen Coupons, und das Kapital gegen Auslieferung der Obligation nebst allen noch nicht fälligen Coupons.

Die fälligen Zinscoupons und Obligationen werden nach Wahl des Inhabers bei der Hongkong and Shanghai Banking Corporation in London in Sterling oder bei der Deutsch-Asiatischen Bank in Berlin und anderen von dieser Bank zu beauftragenden Stellen in Berlin, Hamburg, Frankfurt a. M. und Köln zum jeweiligen Tagescourse für achttägige Sterling-Wechsel auf London bezahlt.

Die vorliegende Obligation ist eine der nachstehend bezeichneten Obligationen gleichen Datums und Inhaltes, nämlich von

30 000	Obligationen Lit. A. zu je £ 25,	No.	1— 30 000	einschliesslich
60 000	„ „ B. „ „ £ 50,	„	1— 60 000	„
110 000	„ „ C. „ „ £ 100,	„	1—110 000	„
2 500	„ „ D. „ „ £ 500,	„	1— 2 500	„

zusammen im Betrage von £ 16 000 000 Sterling.

Die Obligationen Lit. A. zu je £ 25 No. 1—1500, Lit. B. zu je £ 50 No. 1—1500, Lit. C. zu je £ 100 No. 1—66 875, Lit. D. zu je £ 500 No. 1—2400 sind gegengezeichnet in London von der Hongkong and Shanghai Banking Corporation und die Obligationen Lit. A. zu je £ 25 No. 1501—30 000, Lit. B. zu je £ 50 No. 1501—60 000, Lit. C. zu je £ 100 No. 66 876—110 000, Lit. D. zu je £ 500 No. 2401—2500 sind gegengezeichnet in Berlin von der Deutsch-Asiatischen Bank.

Die Ausloosung der Obligationen zur Rückzahlung findet gemäss des denselben aufgedruckten Verloosungsplanes **im Hause der Hongkong and Shanghai Banking Corporation in London** im Laufe des Monats Januar jeden Jahres, erstmalig im Jahre 1899, statt.

Die Kaiserlich Chinesische Regierung hat sich ausdrücklich verpflichtet, die Anleihe weder zu convertiren, noch anders zurückzuzahlen, als in dem Tilgungsplane bestimmt ist.

Die Obligationen und Coupons dieser Anleihe sind von jeder gegenwärtigen und zukünftigen chinesischen Steuer befreit.

Diese Obligation ist auf Grund Kaiserlichen Edicts vom 2. März 1898 in Gemässheit eines Vertrages ausgegeben, welcher in Peking unter dem 1. März 1898 zwischen dem Tsung-Li-Yamên, Namens der Kaiserlich Chinesischen Regierung einerseits und der Hongkong and Shanghai Banking Corporation und der Deutsch-Asiatischen Bank andererseits abgeschlossen worden ist. Ein Auszug aus diesem Vertrage ist auf der Rückseite dieser Obligation abgedruckt.

Zur Beurkundung des Vorstehenden hat entweder Seine Excellenz Chih Chen Lo-Fêng-Luh, Ausserordentlicher Gesandter und Bevollmächtigter Minister Seiner Majestät des Kaisers von China bei Ihrer Majestät der Königin des vereinigten Königreiches von Gross-Britannien und Irland, Kaiserin von Indien, oder Seine Excellenz Lü Tajen, Ausserordentlicher Gesandter und Bevollmächtigter Minister Seiner Majestät des Kaisers von China bei Seiner Majestät dem Deutschen Kaiser hierunter am 1. März 1898 seine Unterschrift und sein Siegel gesetzt.

£ 50

D. No 144.

Deutsch-Asiatische Bank.

德華銀行

Shanghai, 28. Juni 1909. 19

D. A. B.
16 JUL 09
№ 3019

Direction

Deutsch- Asiatische Bank

Berlin

07

07 Letterhead of Deutsch-Asiatische Bank Shanghai.

08 Chinese employees of Deutsch-Asiatische Bank in Shanghai around 1900.

09 Senior executives of Deutsch-Asiatische Bank in Shanghai at an evening event around 1900.

08

09

10

10 200-dollar note of Deutsch-Asiatische Bank from 1914. The front of the note was in German and Chinese, the back in English and Chinese. The banknotes were so popular that Chinese banks started issuing them as well.

11 Deutsch-Asiatische Bank participated in the issue of the Chinese Reorganisation Gold Loan of 1913, as well as a British, French, Japanese and Russian bank.

870314

No

870314

M.2045 oder £100 oder Frs. 2525.

M.2045 oder Rbl. 947 oder Yen 979.60.

THE CHINESE GOVERNMENT

FIVE PER CENT. REORGANISATION GOLD LOAN OF 1913
FOR £25,000,000 STERLING.
£25,000,000 STERLING: OR MARKS 511,250,000: OR FRANCS 631,250,000:
OR ROUBLES 236,750,000: OR YEN 244,900,000.

SCHULDVERSCHREIBUNG ÜBER 2045 MARK
ODER £100 STERLING, ODER 2525 FRANCS, ODER 947 RUBEL, ODER 979.60 YEN.

THE CHINESE GOVERNMENT 5% REORGANISATION GOLD LOAN OF 1913 FOR £25,000,000 STERLING.	5% CHINESISCHE REORGANISATIONS-STAATSANLEIHE IN GOLD VON 1913. ÜBER 511,250,000 MARK.	EMPRUNT DE L'ETAT CHINOIS 5% OR DE 1913. DE RÉORGANISATION DE FRS. 631,250,000.	КИТАЙСКІЙ ПРАВИТЕЛЬСТВЕННЫЙ ПЯТИ-ПРОЦЕНТНЫЙ РЕОРГАНИЗАЦІОННЫЙ ЗОЛОТОЙ ЗАЕМЪ 1913г. НА НАРИЦАТЕЛЬНЫЙ КАПИТАЛЪ 236,750,000 РУБЛЕЙ.
OR MARKS 511,250,000: OR FRANCS 631,250,000: OR ROUBLES 236,750,000: OR YEN 244,900,000.	ODER £25,000,000 STERLING, ODER 631,250,000 FRANCS, ODER 236,750,000 RUBEL, ODER 244,900,000 YEN.	OU £25,000,000 STERLING, OU 511,250,000 MARKS, OU 236,750,000 ROUBLES, OU 244,900,000 YENS.	ИЛИ Ф.СТ. 25,000,000: ИЛИ МАР. 511,250,000: ИЛИ ФРАНК. 631,250,000: ИЛИ ІЕНЪ 244,900,000.
BOND FOR £100.	SCHULDVERSCHREIBUNG ÜBER M.2045.	OBLIGATION DE FRS. 2525.	ОБЛИГАЦІЯ ВЪ 947 РУБЛЕЙ.

GEGENGEZEICHNET ZUM ZWECKE DER IDENTIFIZIERUNG:
DEUTSCH-ASIATISCHE BANK.

中華民國之璽

劉玉麟

11

13

12 The German Club in Shanghai in 1913.

13 Prince Heinrich, the brother of German Emperor Wilhelm II, visited Shanghai in April 1898. The photograph, taken in front of the Shanghai Country Club, shows the prince in a naval officer's uniform in the midst of a gathering of German businessmen.

01

TIENTSIN

01 Temporary premises of Deutsch-Asiatische Bank in Tientsin (now Tianjin) around 1905.

02–03 New building of the Tientsin branch of Deutsch-Asiatische Bank in 1909.

02

03

04

04 Heinrich Cordes managed the Tientsin branch in the first decade of the 20th century. Here, he is shown in the uniform of a lieutenant of the reserve corps.

05 Temporary passport issued by the German Consulate in Tientsin for Richard Lilly, authorized representative ("Prokurist") at Deutsch-Asiatische Bank.

Pass-Journal No. 1339.

DEUTSCHES REICH.

Das Kaiserlich Deutsche Consulat

ersucht hiermit sämmtliche Civil- und Militair-Behörden, Vorzeiger dieses [illegible]

frei und ungehindert reisen, ihm auch nöthigen Falls Schutz und Beistand angedeihen zu lassen [illegible]

Signalement des Pass-Inhabers:

Alter	34 Jahre
Haar	[illegible]
Augen	blau
Nase	[illegible]
Mund	[illegible]
Bart	[illegible]
Statur	[illegible]

Besondere Kennzeichen: [illegible]

Unterschrift des Pass-Inhabers: [illegible]

Gegeben zu Tientsin den 16. Juli 1900

[illegible] Kaiserlich[e] Konsul

Zimmermann

KAISERLICH DEUTSCHES CONSULAT IN TIENTSIN

Ausgefertigt auf [illegible]

Gültig für 6 Wochen.

Gesehen.
Usedom
Kapitän zur See Kommandant der deutschen Streitkräfte zu Tientsin

01

02

HANKOW

01 Deutsch-Asiatische Bank in Hankow (now part of Wuhan) In 1906.

02 Hermann Wolff, manager of the Hankow agency, with Chinese employees in 1899.

03 Map of Hankow around 1900.

HANKOW
(口漢)
With
HANYANG AND WUCHANG
(昌武及陽漢)
Scale 1 : 40,000
Japanese Ri
Chinese Li
English Mile
Kilometers
WUCHANG
(昌武)
HANYANG
(陽漢)
L. Sha-hu
L. Yüeh-hu
L. Lien-hwa-hu
Japanese Cemetery
Race Course
Golf Club
Chinese Race Course
Hupeh Agricultural College
Barracks of XVI Brigade
Barracks of XV Brigade
Military Primary School
Hanyang Arsenal
Hanyang Iron and Steel Works
Cotton Spinning and Weaving Factory
Canton-Hankow Railway Office
PEKING HANKOW RAILWAY
JAPANESE CONCESSION
GERMAN CONCESSION
FRENCH CONCESSION
RUSSIAN CONCESSION
BRITISH CONCESSION

01

TSING-TAO

01 View of Tsing-Tao (now Qingdao), the capital city of the German protectorate Kiautchou, in 1913.

02 The Tsing-Tao branch of Deutsch-Asiatische Bank was opened in 1898.

02

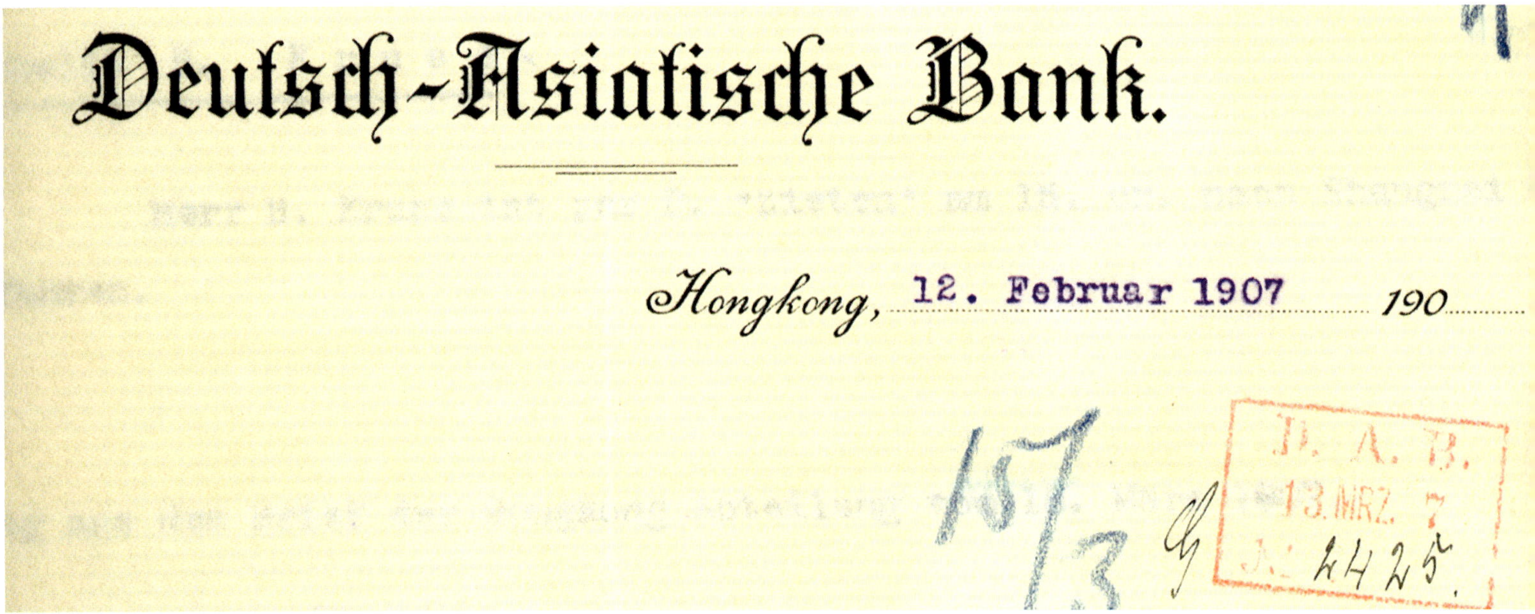
Deutsch-Asiatische Bank.

Hongkong, 12. Februar 1907 190

D. A. B.
13. MRZ. 7
№ 2425.

01

HONG KONG

01 Letterhead of Deutsch-Asiatische Bank in Hong Kong.

02 Deutsch-Asiatische Bank in Hong Kong in 1914.

02

03

03 Deutsch-Asiatische Bank in the British Crown Colony in 1914.

04 After the beginning of the First World War, the Hong Kong branch was placed under official supervision. The building was put up for auction in 1915 shortly after completion and converted in 1918 as these plans show.

05 Workplaces at Deutsch-Asiatische Bank in Hong Kong.

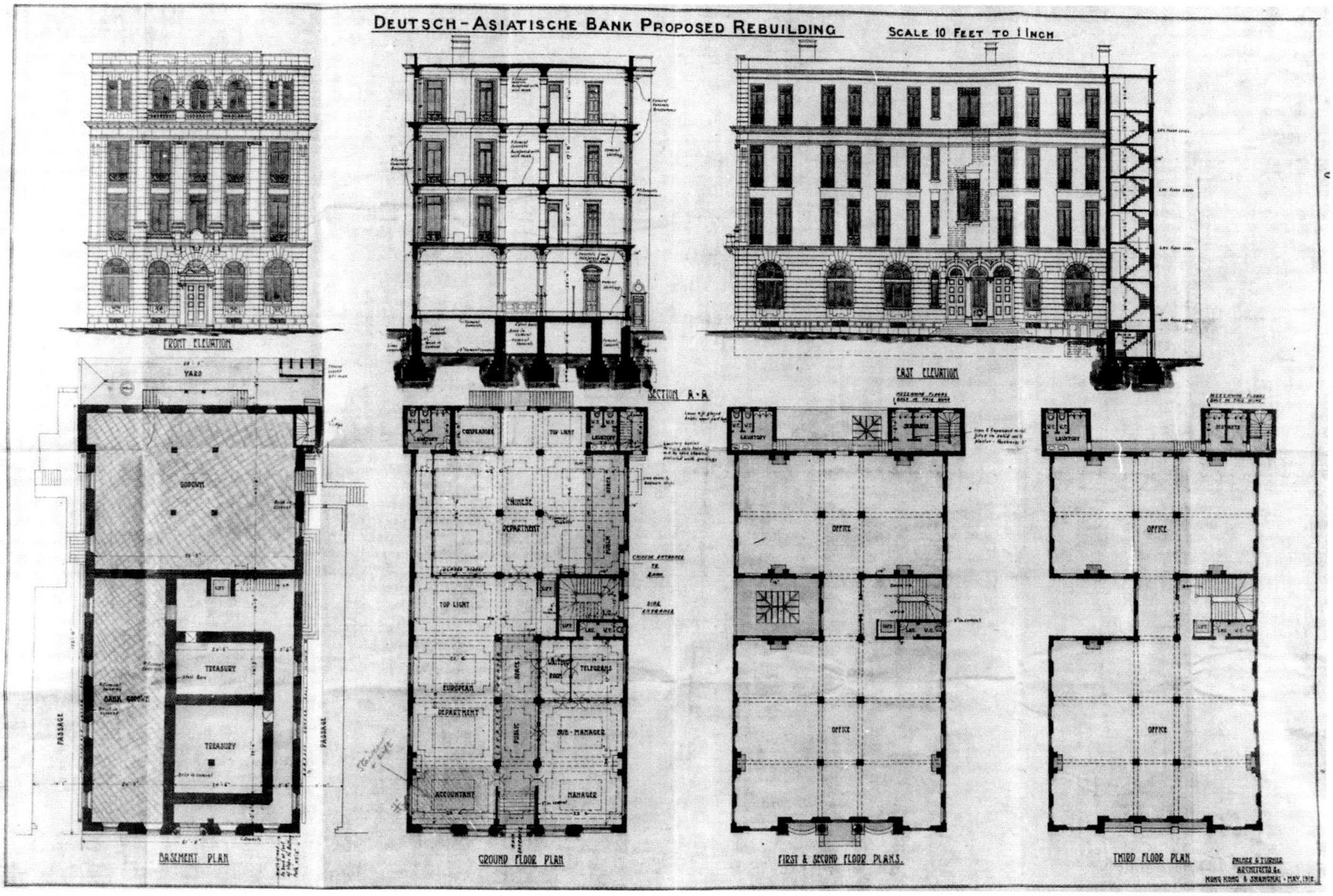
DEUTSCH-ASIATISCHE BANK PROPOSED REBUILDING
SCALE 10 FEET TO 1 INCH
FRONT ELEVATION
SECTION A-A
EAST ELEVATION
BASEMENT PLAN
GROUND FLOOR PLAN
FIRST & SECOND FLOOR PLANS
THIRD FLOOR PLAN
PASSAGE
TREASURY
CHINESE DEPARTMENT
EUROPEAN DEPARTMENT
ACCOUNTANT
SUB-MANAGER
MANAGER
OFFICE

04

05

01

TSINANFU

01 The Tsinanfu (now Jinan) branch of Deutsch-Asiatische Bank was opened in 1904.

01

PEKING

01 In Peking (now Beijing), Deutsch-Asiatische Bank set up an agency in 1905 and upgraded it to a branch in 1910. In 1906, the Peking branch built its own elegant offices featuring an impressive corner tower.

02

02 Entrance to the Peking branch.

03 Closure of the Peking branch in August 1917.

04 Five-tael banknote of Deutsch-Asiatische Bank in Peking.

03

04

5 TAEL 両伍
5 TAEL 両伍
德華銀行
№ 10251
BANKNOTE
über 5 TAEL
FÜNF TAEL
PEKING WÄHRUNG zahlt die
DEUTSCH-ASIATISCHE BANK
dem Einlieferer dieser Banknote an ihrer hiesigen Kasse.
PEKING, den 1. März 1907.
DEUTSCH-ASIATISCHE BANK.
伍両
京平足銀伍両
京 PEKING 北
№ 10251
京 PEKING 北

01

CANTON

01 The Canton (now Guangzhou) branch of Deutsch-Asiatische Bank was opened in 1910.

SHANTUNG RAILWAY COMPANY

01 Map of the Province of Shantung (Shandong) showing the railways and coal areas around 1900.

01

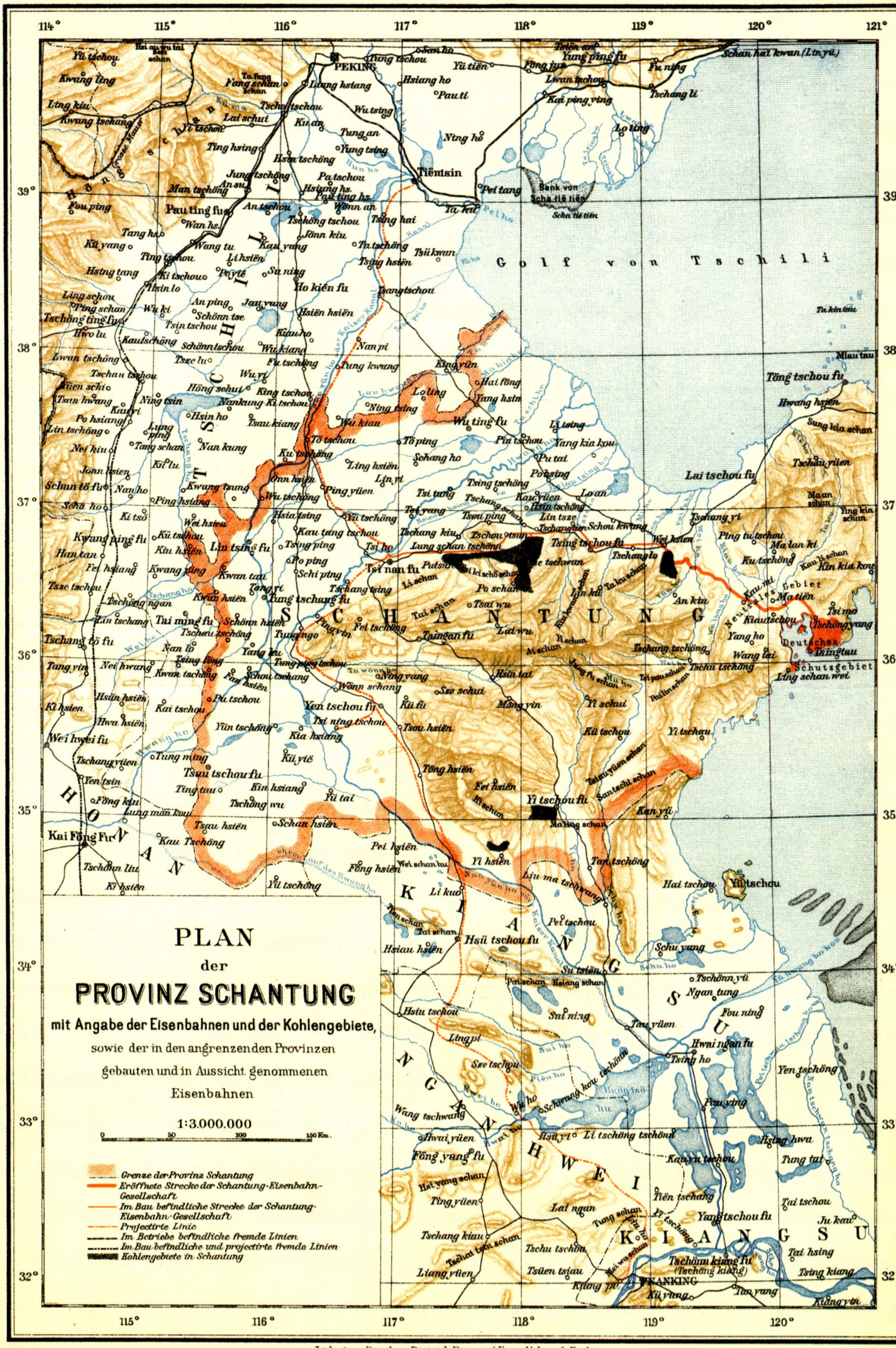

Lithogr. u. Druck v. Dietrich Reimer [Ernst Vohsen] Berlin

02

03

Telegr.-Adresse:
ANTUNG BERLIN.
rnsprecher: Amt I, 1880.

Schantung-Eisenbahn-Gesellschaft.

EINGEGANGEN AM
1151 * 31. MAI. 1902
DEUTSCHE BANK

VII

Berlin W., 64, den 31. Mai 1902
Behrenstrasse 14–16 II.

An die

DEUTSCHE BANK

Berlin.

04

02 Group of surveyors from the Shantung Railway Company around 1900.

03 Letterhead of Shantung Railway Company, founded in 1899 under the management of Deutsch-Asiatische Bank.

04 Railway station of the Shantung Railway Company.

05 Opening of the Tsing-Tao-Kiautchou-Tsinanfu railway on June 1, 1904.

06

07

08

06 Shantung Railway Company train decorated with flags for a test ride.

07 German and Chinese dignitaries about to board a Shantung Railway Company train.

08 German and Chinese dignitaries in a saloon car of the Shantung Railway Company.

德華銀行

D-A-B

DEUTSCH-ASIATISCHE BANK
1925–1945

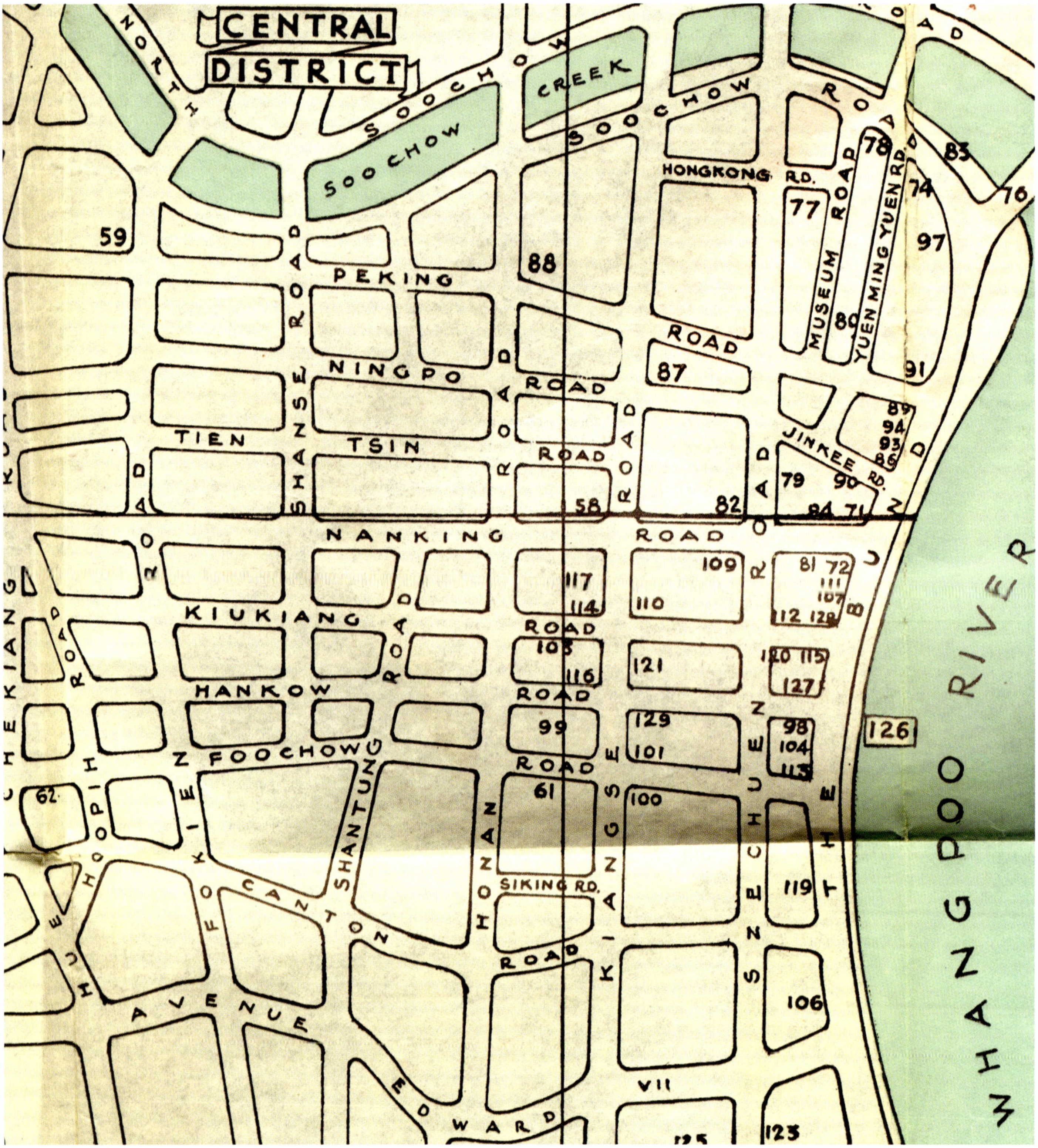
CENTRAL
DISTRICT
SOOCHOW CREEK
SOOCHOW
SOOCHOW ROAD
NORTH
HONGKONG RD.
MUSEUM ROAD
YUEN MING YUEN RD.
PEKING ROAD
NINGPO ROAD
TIEN TSIN ROAD
JINKEE RD.
NANKING ROAD
KIUKIANG ROAD
HANKOW ROAD
FOOCHOW ROAD
CANTON ROAD
SIKING RD.
AVENUE EDWARD
SHANSE ROAD
SHANTUNG
HONAN
KIANGSE
SZECHUEN ROAD
THE BUND
CHEKIANG
HOOPIH
FOKIEN
HUPEH
WHANGPOO RIVER
59
88
77
78
83
74
76
97
80
87
91
89
94
93
85
79
90
84
71
58
82
109
81
72
111
107
117
114
110
112
128
108
116
121
120
115
127
99
129
101
98
104
113
126
61
100
62
119
106
123
01

02

SHANGHAI

01 A map of the central district in Shanghai around 1930.

02 The "Bund" in Shanghai around 1930.

03

03 The Deutsch-Asiatische Bank building in Shanghai at 85 Kiukiang Road around 1930.

04 Site map of Deutsch-Asiatische Bank in Shanghai.

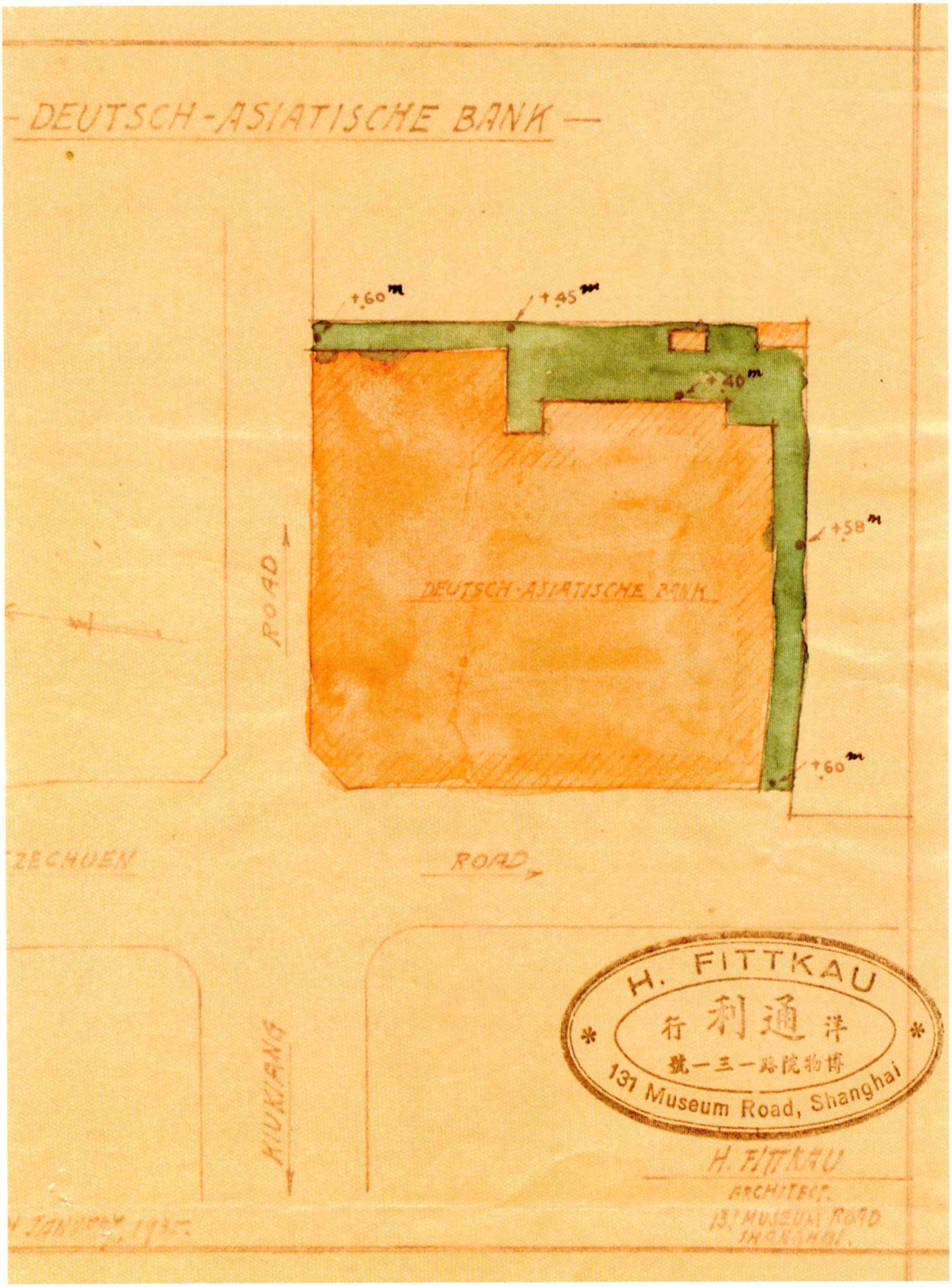
DEUTSCH-ASIATISCHE BANK
+.60m
+.45m
+.40m
+.58m
+.60m
DEUTSCH-ASIATISCHE BANK
ROAD
ZECHUEN
ROAD
KIUKIANG
H. FITTKAU
洋通利行
博物院路一三一號
131 Museum Road, Shanghai
H. FITTKAU
ARCHITECT
131 MUSEUM ROAD
SHANGHAI

04

05

06

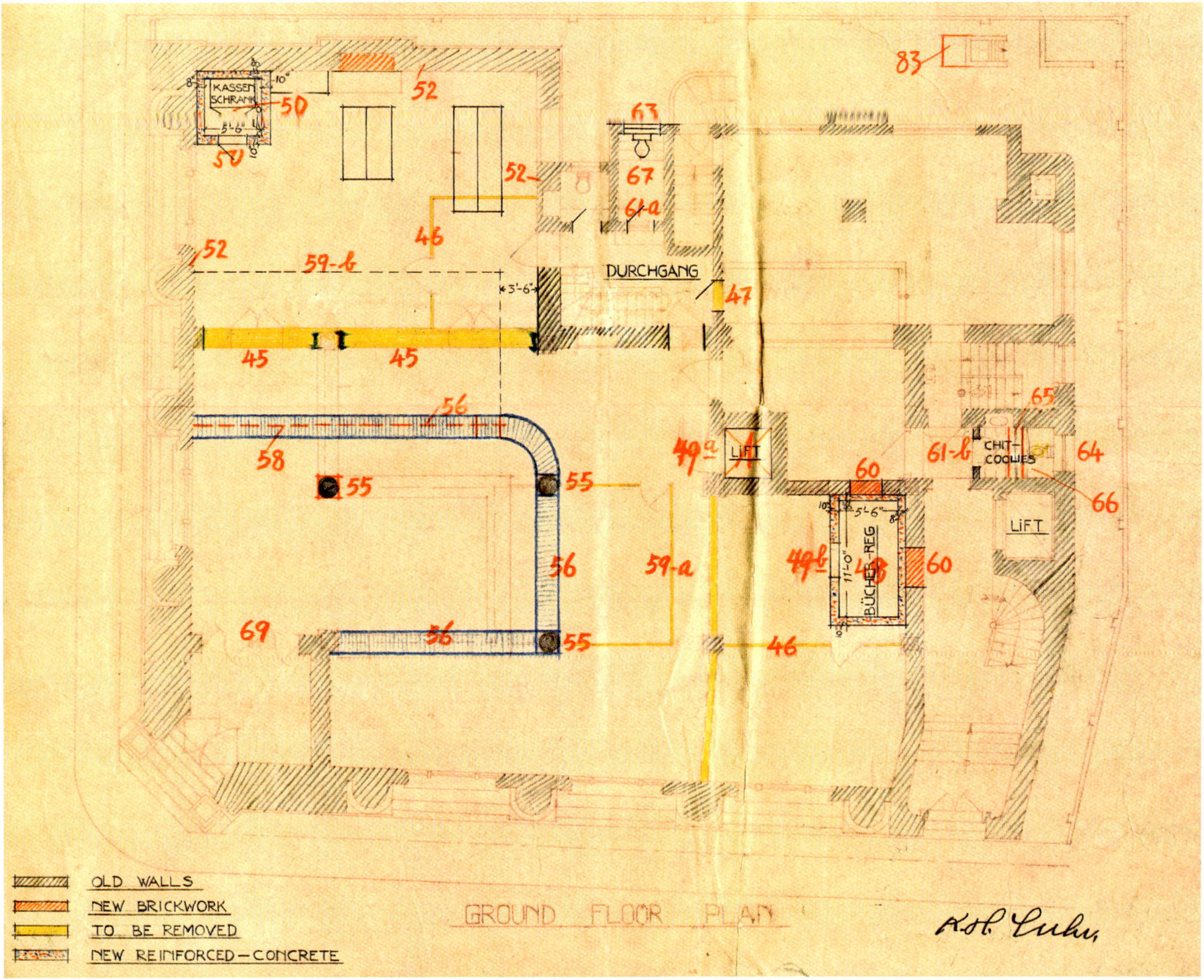
KASSEN SCHRANK
DURCHGANG
LIFT
CHIT-COOLIES
BÜCHER-REG
LIFT
OLD WALLS
NEW BRICKWORK
TO BE REMOVED
NEW REINFORCED-CONCRETE
GROUND FLOOR PLAN

TELEGRAM-ADDRESS:
TEUTONIA SHANGHAI

TELEPHONE:
11536 (4 LINES)
PRIVATE EXCHANGE TO ALL DEPTS.
12772 MANAGER ONLY

P. O. BOX NO. 1282.

D No.197

Deutsch-Asiatische Bank.

德華銀行

D. A. B.
№ 00129 ★ 10.JAN.1934
DIREKTION

Kl/Le

7 KIUKIANG ROAD.

SHANGHAI, 13.Dezember 1933

Direktion der Deutsch-Asiatischen Bank,
Berlin

07

05 The banking hall of Deutsch-Asiatische Bank in Shanghai around 1930.

06 Floor plan of the ground floor of Deutsch-Asiatische Bank in Shanghai around 1930.

07 Letterhead of Deutsch-Asiatische Bank in Shanghai from 1933.

德華銀行
Tuck-hwa-ying-hong
DEUTSCH-ASIATISCHE BANK
(German)
294 Szechuen Rd. P.O.B. 1282
T. 11536 & 12772 (Mgr.)
T. A. "Teutonia"

Reiss, A., *mgr.*
Mirow, E., *sub-mgr.*
Knoke, W., *sub-mgr.*
Fischer, K. H., *dep. sub-mgr.*
Loeffler, H., *dep. sub-mgr.*
Scheeffer, E., *signs p.p.*
Klussmann, M.
Meyer-Buete, G.
Kleinschmidt, H.
Witting, Dr. P.
Dietsch, H.
Bretschneider, F.
Link, E.
Munz, K.
Hoppe, Miss E.
Lehmann, Miss E.

Head Office:—Shanghai
Branches:—
Berlin, Canton, Hamburg, Hankow, Peiping, Tientsin & Tsingtau

08

09

10

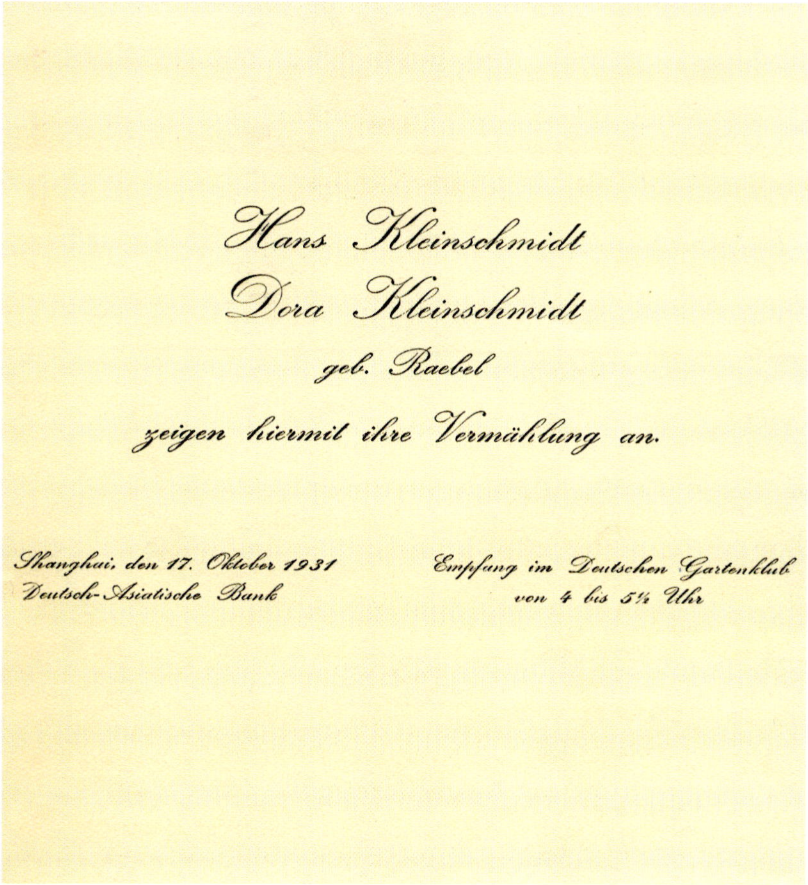

Hans Kleinschmidt
Dora Kleinschmidt
geb. Raebel
zeigen hiermit ihre Vermählung an.

Shanghai, den 17. Oktober 1931
Deutsch-Asiatische Bank

Empfang im Deutschen Gartenklub
von 4 bis 5½ Uhr

11

08 Entry of Deutsch-Asiatische Bank in Shanghai in the Credit Men's Business Directory of China from 1934.

09 Hans Loeffler was with Deutsch-Asiatische Bank in East Asia from 1921 to 1945, in the mid-1930s as deputy sub-manager in Shanghai. The photograph was taken in 1922 in Yokohama, the location of his first assignment.

10 In 1923, following an apprenticeship at Deutsche Bank, Hans Kleinschmidt joined Deutsch-Asiatische Bank, which sent him in 1927 to Shanghai, where he worked until 1936. Subsequently, he was transferred to the Canton branch.

11 Announcement of the marriage of Hans and Dora Kleinschmidt from 1931.

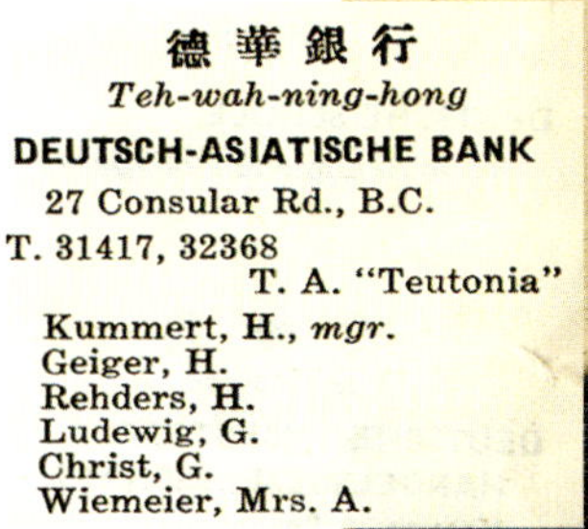
德華銀行
Teh-wah-ning-hong
DEUTSCH-ASIATISCHE BANK
27 Consular Rd., B.C.
T. 31417, 32368
T. A. "Teutonia"
Kummert, H., *mgr.*
Geiger, H.
Rehders, H.
Ludewig, G.
Christ, G.
Wiemeier, Mrs. A.

01

02

03

德華銀行
Tuck-hwa-ying-hong
DEUTSCH-ASIATISCHE BANK
2 Kwan Tao Rd. P.O.B. 1
T. 2954 T. A. "Teutoni
Koch, H., *mgr.*
Ewert, Rudolf
Schmollinger, Oskar
Dienel, A.

04

TIENTSIN AND TSING-TAO

01 Entry of the Tientsin branch of Deutsch-Asiatische Bank in the China Business Directory from 1934.

02 Gerhard Ludewig joined Deutsch-Asiatische Bank in 1927 in Shanghai; after working for a time In Hankow, he moved to the Tientsin branch in 1934.

03 Oskar Schmollinger came to China in 1930, first joining the Tsing-Tao branch and then working at Deutsch-Asiatische Bank in Shanghai from 1935 to 1945.

04 Entry of the Tsing-Tao branch of Deutsch-Asiatische Bank in the China Business Directory from 1934.

05 Advertisement for Deutsch-Asiatische Bank in Shanghai around 1930.

DEUTSCH-ASIATISCHE BANK

GEGRÜNDET 1889
AKTIEN KAPITAL
YUAN 6.440.000.00

IN SHANGHAI
85 KIUKIANG ROAD

GEGRÜNDET 1889
RESERVEN
YUAN 2.044.000.00

FILIALEN IN DEUTSCHLAND:

BERLIN N.W.7. MITTELSTRASSE 2-4 HAMBURG 1, LOMBARDSBRÜCKE 1

FILIALEN IN CHINA:

KANTON - HANKAU - PEIPING - TIENTSIN - TSINGTAO

Telegr. Adresse: für Berlin und Hamburg
CHINABANK

Telegr. Adresse: für Filialen in China
TEUTONIA

德 華 銀 行

行址・設於上海・創立年期一八八九年

資　　本：六百四十四萬元
準 備 金：二百零四萬四千元

分行所在地

Berlin N. W. 7, Mittelstrasse 2-4　　Hamburg 1, Lombardsbruecke 1

廣州　漢口　北平　天津　青島

電報掛號：在柏林與漢堡用：Chinabank　在中國各地分行用：Teutonia.

業務　業務辦理各種銀行業務：
國內外定期存款
電信滙兌
經理往來賬目
賣買及收理各種證券
發行各種支票及信用狀

下列各銀行及銀公司指定爲本銀行董事會之代表

Berliner Handelsgesellschaft, Berlin. - S. Bleichroeder, Berlin, - Deutsche Bank und Disconto - Gesellschaft, Berlin, - Dresdner Bank, - Mendelssohn & Co., Berlin, - Jacob S. H. Stern Frankfurt a. M., - Sal. Oppenheim jr. & Cie., Koeln, - Bayerische Hypotheken - und Wechsel - Bank, Muenchen.

05

DAB

DEUTSCH-ASIATISCHE BANK
1945–1972

01

HAMBURG

01 Staff of Deutsch-Asiatische Bank at a Christmas party in the Ratsweinkeller Hamburg in 1952.

02 In 1954, Deutsch-Asiatische Bank moved into a new building in Hamburg.

DEUTSCH-
ASIATISCHE
BANK DAB
HANSEATISCHE VON 1826
ELEKTRO
WULFF
MOSER

02

01

02

HONG KONG

01 Hong Kong in the 1950s.

02 Entrance of the Hong Kong branch of Deutsch-Asiatische Bank at St. George's Building.

03

03 Office scene in the Hong Kong branch of Deutsch-Asiatische Bank in 1958.

04

04 Counter at the Hong Kong branch of Deutsch-Asiatische Bank in 1958.

05 Counter of the Hong Kong branch of Deutsch-Asiatische Bank in 1964.

06 Bookkeeping at the Hong Kong branch of Deutsch-Asiatische Bank in 1964.

05

06

EUROPEAN ASIAN BANK AND DEUTSCHE BANK (ASIA) 1972–1988

01

大酒樓
GOLDEN GLORY
RESTAURANT
NAINANI'S
CUSTOM TAILORS
ON PARLE FRANÇAIS
荔香村酒家
CHARLES & CO.
INENS & NOVELTIES
LEE PIANO CO. LTD
神戸時計店
KOBE WATCH CO.
行銀亞歐
European Asian Bank
Agina
BEAUTY HOUSE
ART CO.
ONG
RIK
REST
PHOTO SALON
FURNITURE
02

03

01 The European Asian Bank headquarters in Hamburg in 1981.

02 Hong Kong street scene with a billboard advertising European Asian Bank.

04

03–04 In 1981, the Aberdeen branch was opened in Hong Kong, one of European Asian Bank's peak total of eight branches in the city.

05

05–06 Advertisements for European Asian Bank from 1978 (left) and 1982 (right).

Lufthansa Cargo
Efficiency. Business in Asia has undergone sweeping changes away from the historical pattern of commodities shipped West and manufactured goods shipped East. With growing diversification and sophistication the economies of Asia have become strongly export-oriented.
As a result speed and efficiency in banking on a worldwide scale have become a vital need for a demanding clientele.
Eurasbank has built a reputation for efficiency during the past decade. Quick documentary transactions. Fast decisions on financing. Sound advice on project finance. Immediate access to a broad branch network in Asia linked to a strong base in Europe.
Eurasbank means efficiency, in any currency.
Hamburg · Bangkok
Bombay · Colombo
Hongkong · Jakarta
Karachi · Kuala Lumpur
Manila · Seoul
Singapore
Taipei · Sydney
Head Office:
Neuer Wall 50
D-2000 Hamburg 36
Telephone 3 61 46-0
Telex 2 162 228 eur d
European Asian Bank
The European bank for business in Asia

06

Deutsche Bank (Asia)
Aktiengesellschaft

DM 196,000,000,-

18.799 Aktien zu je DM 10.000,-
Nr. 000001 - 18.799

und

8.010 Aktien zu je DM 1.000,-
Nr. 000001 - 8.010

GLOBALNAMENSAKTIE
über
Einhundertsechsundneunzig Millionen Deutsche Mark
eingeteilt in 18.799 Namensaktien zu je nom. DM 10.000,-
und 8.010 Namensaktien zu je nom. DM 1.000,-

Die Deutsche Bank Aktiengesellschaft, Frankfurt am Main, ist mit dieser Globalnamensaktie bei der Deutsche Bank (Asia) Aktiengesellschaft, Hamburg, nach Maßgabe der Satzung als Aktionär beteiligt. Diese Aktie kann gemäß § 5 der Satzung nur mit Zustimmung der Gesellschaft übertragen werden.

Hamburg, im Oktober 1987

Deutsche Bank (Asia)
Aktiengesellschaft

Eingetragen im Aktienbuch
Band 2 Seite 4

Der Aufsichtsrat
Vo[illegible]ender

Der Vorstand

Kontrollbeamter

07

07 Registered share of Deutsche Bank (Asia), which had emerged from European Asian Bank at the end of 1986.

08 Announcement of the renaming of European Asian Bank as Deutsche Bank (Asia).

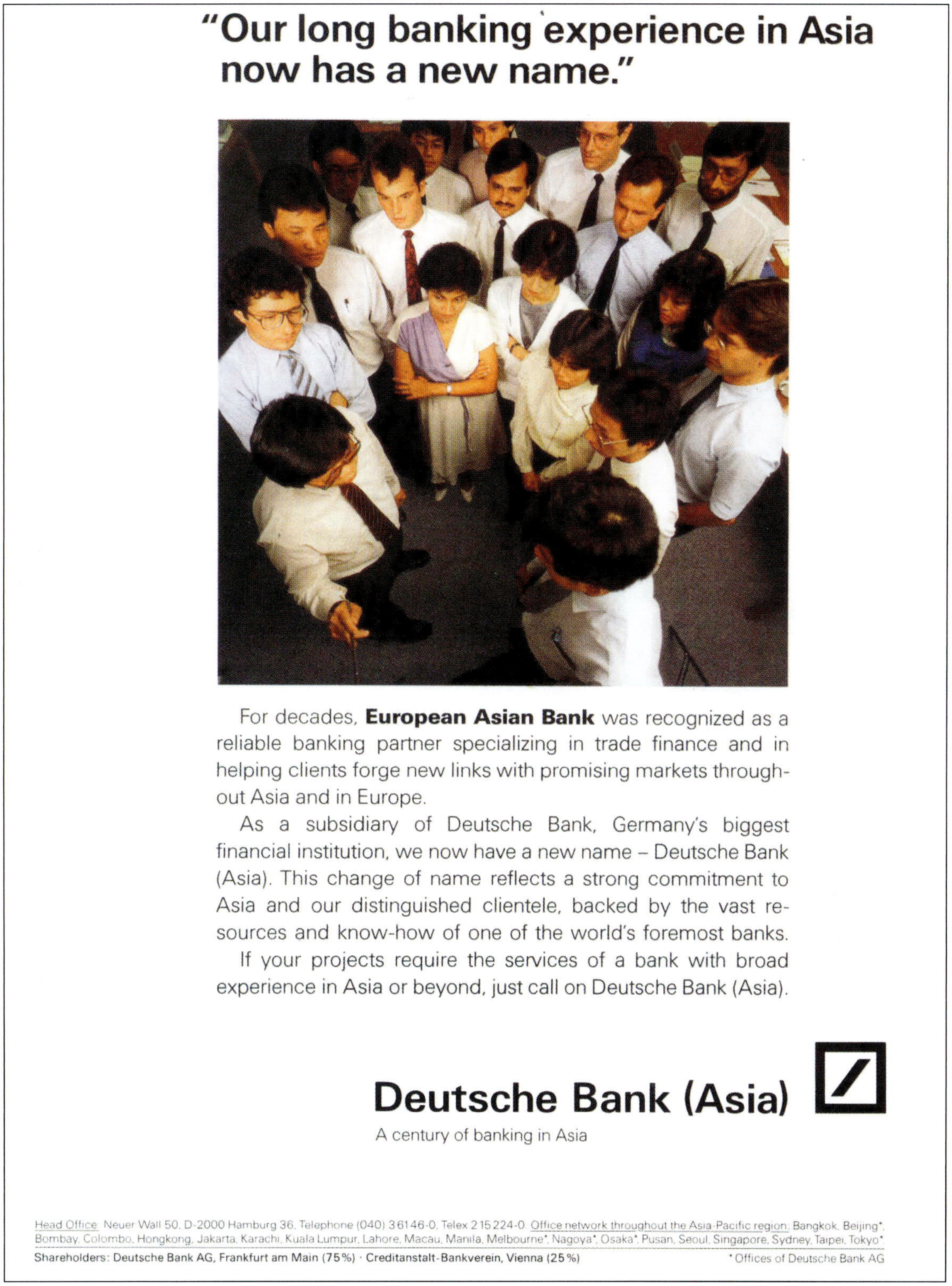
"Our long banking experience in Asia now has a new name."
For decades, **European Asian Bank** was recognized as a reliable banking partner specializing in trade finance and in helping clients forge new links with promising markets throughout Asia and in Europe.
As a subsidiary of Deutsche Bank, Germany's biggest financial institution, we now have a new name – Deutsche Bank (Asia). This change of name reflects a strong commitment to Asia and our distinguished clientele, backed by the vast resources and know-how of one of the world's foremost banks.
If your projects require the services of a bank with broad experience in Asia or beyond, just call on Deutsche Bank (Asia).
Deutsche Bank (Asia)
A century of banking in Asia
Head Office: Neuer Wall 50, D-2000 Hamburg 36, Telephone (040) 36146-0, Telex 215224-0. Office network throughout the Asia-Pacific region: Bangkok, Beijing*, Bombay, Colombo, Hongkong, Jakarta, Karachi, Kuala Lumpur, Lahore, Macau, Manila, Melbourne*, Nagoya*, Osaka*, Pusan, Seoul, Singapore, Sydney, Taipei, Tokyo*
Shareholders: Deutsche Bank AG, Frankfurt am Main (75%) · Creditanstalt-Bankverein, Vienna (25%)
* Offices of Deutsche Bank AG

08

DEUTSCHE BANK IN CHINA
1976–2008

Deutsche Bank

01

02

Deutsche Bank
Regional Representative Office

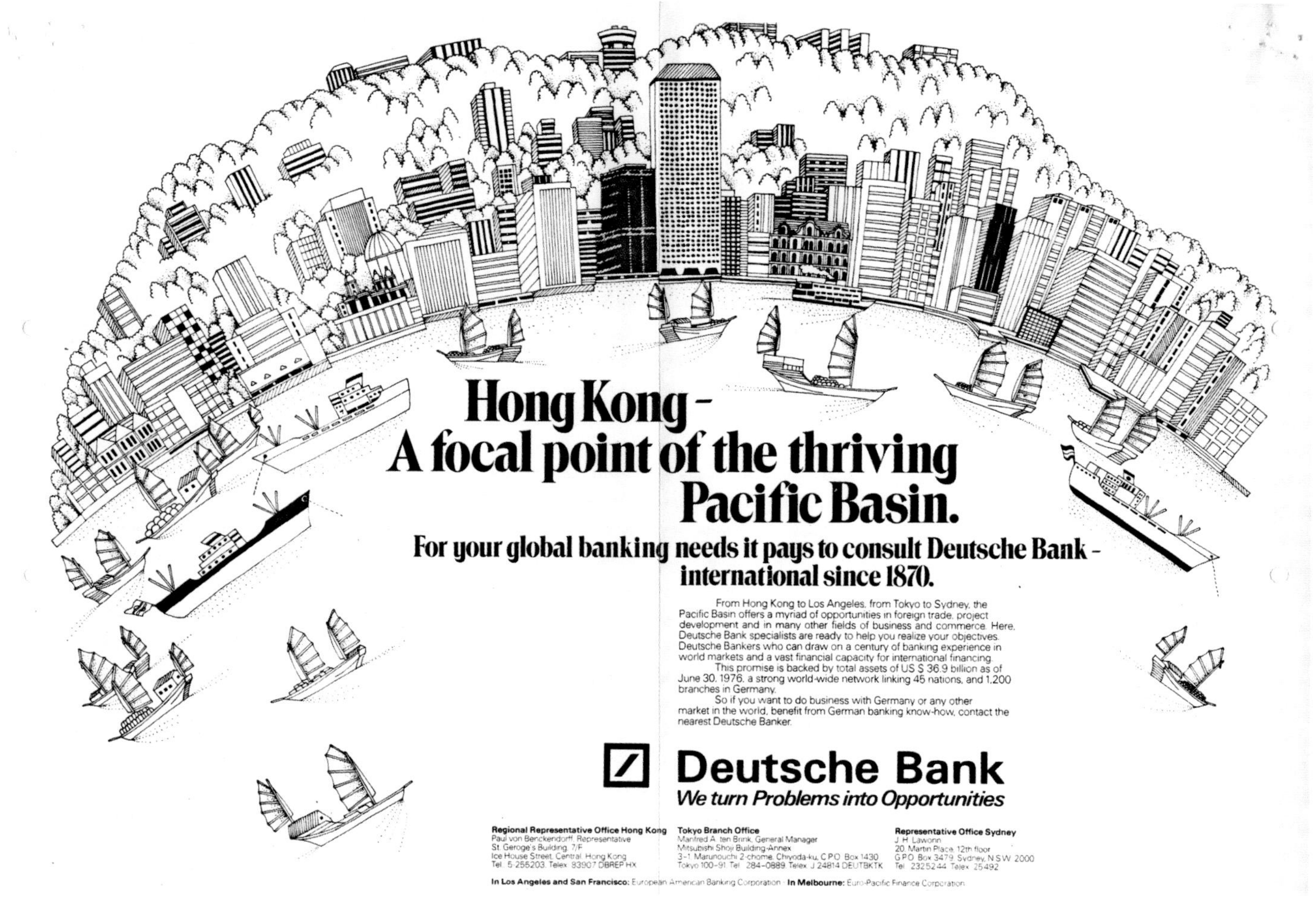

03

HONG KONG

01–02 Parallel to the European Asian Bank in Hong Kong, Deutsche Bank opened its own regional representative office in the city in 1976.

03 Advertisement of the opening of the regional representative office in Hong Kong in 1976.

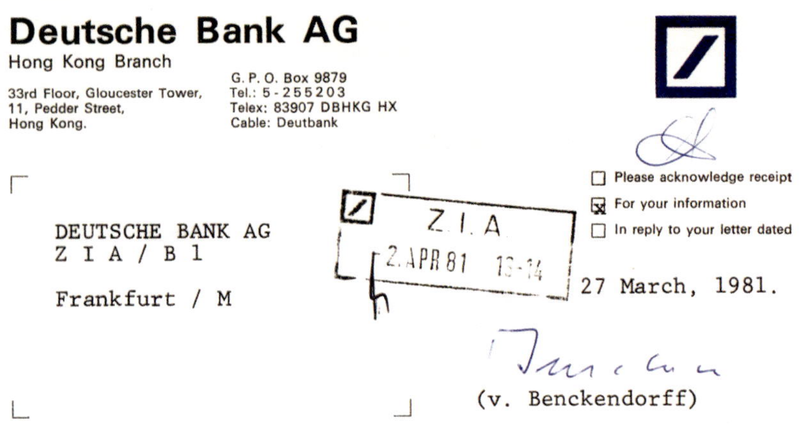

Deutsche Bank AG
Hong Kong Branch

33rd Floor, Gloucester Tower,
11, Pedder Street,
Hong Kong.

G. P. O. Box 9879
Tel.: 5-255203
Telex: 83907 DBHKG HX
Cable: Deutbank

DEUTSCHE BANK AG
Z I A / B 1

Frankfurt / M

Z.I.A
2.APR 81 13-14

☐ Please acknowledge receipt
☒ For your information
☐ In reply to your letter dated

27 March, 1981.

(v. Benckendorff)

04

05

04 Letterhead of Deutsche Bank's Hong Kong branch, which emerged in 1979 from the regional representative office.

05 Office in Deutsche Bank's Hong Kong branch in 1979.

06 Today, Deutsche Bank Hong Kong is located in the Cheung Kong Center. The bank has over 1,300 employees in the Special Administrative Region of China.

06

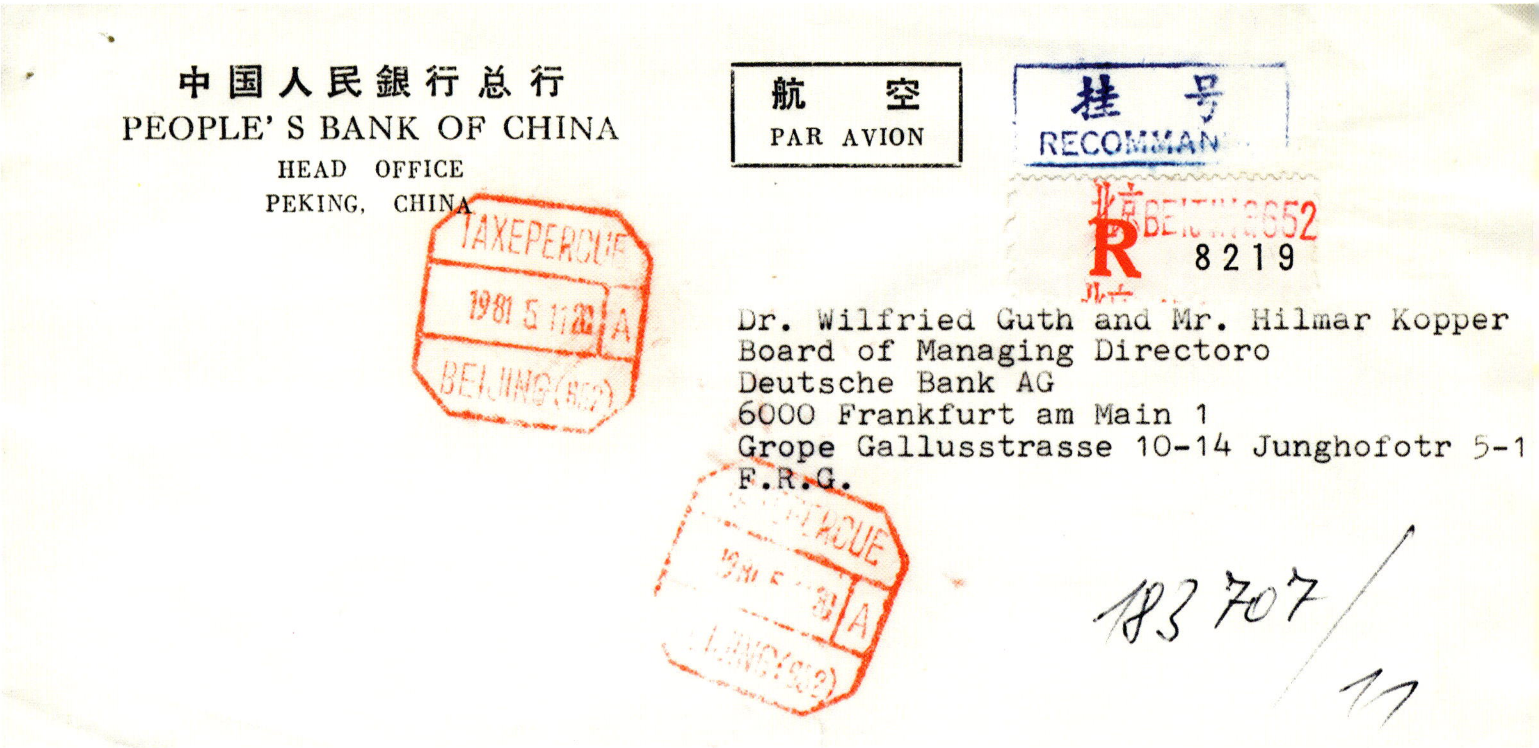

01

BEIJING

01–02 Letter from the President of the People's Bank of China, Li Baohua, dated May 8, 1981, to the Management Board, authorizing the opening of a Deutsche Bank representative office in Beijing.

中國人民銀行

德意志银行

董事会W·古特博士、H·科佩尔先生：

一九八〇年十一月二十七日，关于申请在我国设立德意志银行北京代表处的来函及所附的有关资料均已收悉。我现在高兴地通知您，贵行已被批准在北京开设代表处。

贵行与我国金融界有着友好密切的合作关系，在开展中德两国金融和贸易往来方面起了积极的作用。谨祝贵行今后为进一步加强两国金融合作，促进双方贸易发展和两国人民的友谊作出更大的贡献。

顺　致

崇高的敬礼！

中国人民银行行长

李葆华

一九八一年五月八日

02

03

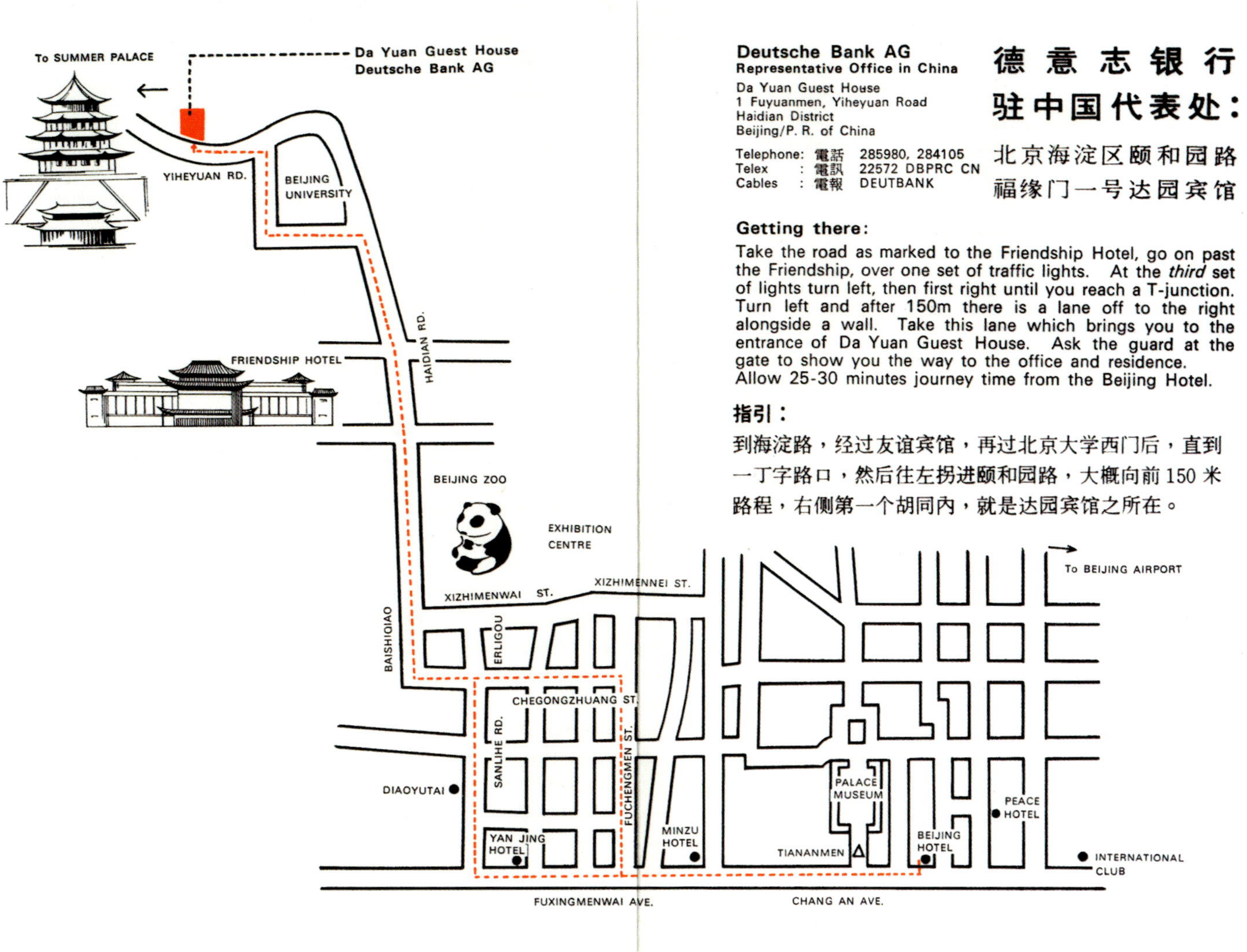

04

03 With the representative office in Beijing, opened by Management Board Spokesman Wilfried Guth in September 1981, Deutsche Bank was the first German bank to be represented in the People's Republic of China.

04 Map showing how to get from the Beijing Hotel to Deutsche Bank's representative office in Beijing.

05

06

07

05 Deutsche Bank's representative office in Beijing in the 1980s.

06 Honorary Chairman of Deutsche Bank, Hermann Josef Abs, and the representative of Deutsche Bank in China, Johannes Schoeter, at the entrance to the bank's premises in Beijing, 1984.

07 Advertisement about the opening of the representative office in Beijing in 1981.

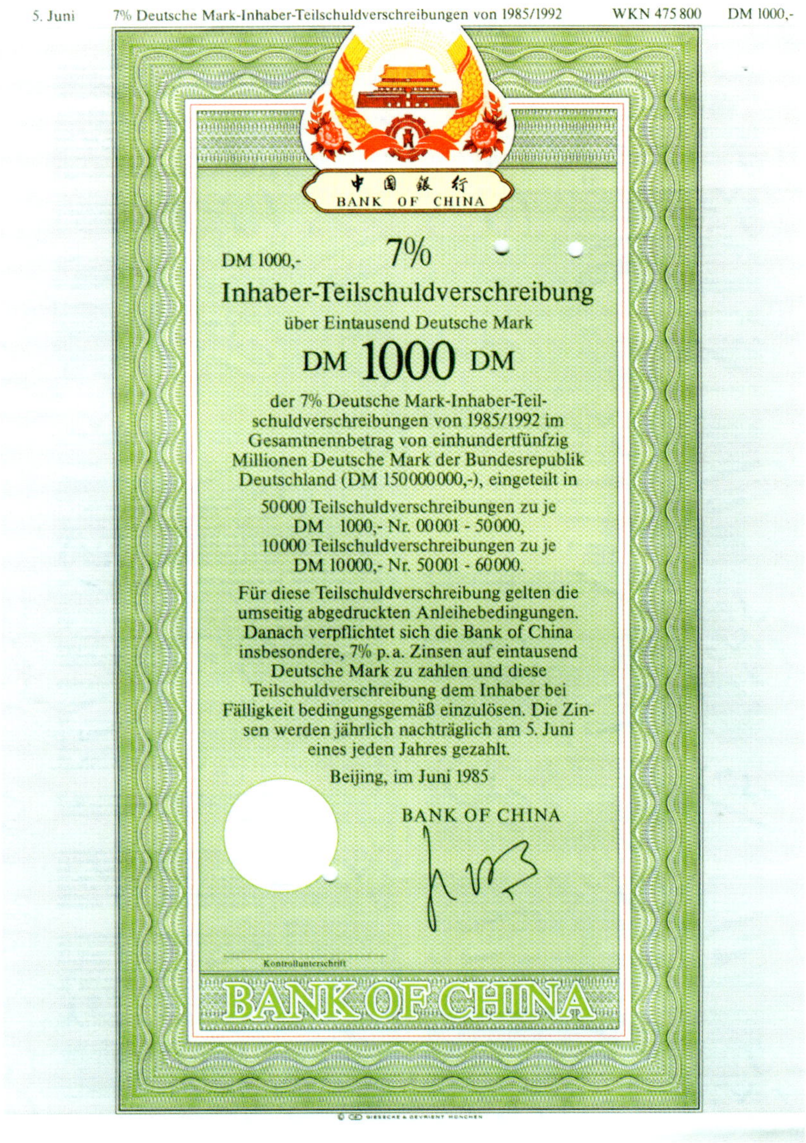

5. Juni 7% Deutsche Mark-Inhaber-Teilschuldverschreibungen von 1985/1992 WKN 475 800 DM 1000,-

中国银行
BANK OF CHINA

DM 1000,- 7%

Inhaber-Teilschuldverschreibung
über Eintausend Deutsche Mark

DM 1000 DM

der 7% Deutsche Mark-Inhaber-Teilschuldverschreibungen von 1985/1992 im Gesamtnennbetrag von einhundertfünfzig Millionen Deutsche Mark der Bundesrepublik Deutschland (DM 150000000,-), eingeteilt in

50000 Teilschuldverschreibungen zu je DM 1000,- Nr. 00001 - 50000,
10000 Teilschuldverschreibungen zu je DM 10000,- Nr. 50001 - 60000.

Für diese Teilschuldverschreibung gelten die umseitig abgedruckten Anleihebedingungen. Danach verpflichtet sich die Bank of China insbesondere, 7% p.a. Zinsen auf eintausend Deutsche Mark zu zahlen und diese Teilschuldverschreibung dem Inhaber bei Fälligkeit bedingungsgemäß einzulösen. Die Zinsen werden jährlich nachträglich am 5. Juni eines jeden Jahres gezahlt.

Beijing, im Juni 1985

BANK OF CHINA

Kontrollunterschrift

BANK OF CHINA

08 In 1985, Deutsche Bank issued a bond of the Bank of China for DM 150 million.

09 Brochure advertising Deutsche Bank as an international partner for Chinese customers in 1990.

10

10 Hilmar Kopper, Spokesman of Deutsche Bank's Management Board (right), and Otto Wolff von Amerongen (centre) meet Zhu Rongji (left), Vice Premier and later Prime Minister of the People's Republic of China, as members of a business delegation to Beijing in 1993.

11

11 In March 2007, the Private & Business Clients branch in Beijing was opened by Peter Schedl (then Head of Private & Business Clients Asia Pacific), George Wang (Head of Private & Business Clients China) and Rainer Neske (Global Head of Private & Business Clients), pictured from left to right.

12 Advertisement for Deutsche Bank (China) from 2008.

CORPORATE & INVESTMENT BANKING
ASSET MANAGEMENT
PRIVATE WEALTH MANAGEMENT
PRIVATE & BUSINESS CLIENTS
1872年在华首家分行
2008年在华设立子行
A Passion to Perform.
Deutsche Bank
德意志银行
详情请浏览www.db.com/china。本广告已获德意志银行批准，由其传达，并纯粹供纪录而已。本广告所述服务由德意志银行或其附属公司及/或关联公司根据当地适用的法律及规定提供。
德意志银行2008版权所有©

13

13 Private & Business Clients staff in Beijing in March 2007.

14 At the beginning of 2008, the new Deutsche Bank (China) Co., Ltd., commenced business in the Huamao building in Beijing's Chao Yang District.

Deutsche Bank
VERSACE
UCCI

01

SHANGHAI

01 The Shanghai branch of Deutsche Bank (China) Co., Ltd., in the AZIA Center.

GUANGZHOU

01 The Guangzhou branch of Deutsche Bank (China) Co., Ltd., in Teem Building, 2008.

01

01

HUA XIA BANK

01 Head office of Hua Xia Bank in Beijing. In October 2005, Deutsche Bank acquired a strategic stake in China's 12th largest bank based on total assets.

02 Ceremony for the signing of the basic agreements between Deutsche Bank and Hua Xia Bank in Beijing on October 17, 2005. Members of the Deutsche Bank delegation pictured in the first row, from right to left: Lee Zhang (Chairman of Deutsche Bank China), Colin Grassie (CEO of Deutsche Bank Asia-Pacific), Richard Walker (General Counsel), Axel Wieandt (Head of Corporate Development) and Rainer Neske (Global Head of Deutsche Bank Private & Business Clients).

03 On November 10, 2005, Josef Ackermann (right), Chairman of the Management Board and the Group Executive Committee of Deutsche Bank, and Liu Haiyan, Chairman of Hua Xia Bank, signed a Comprehensive Long-Term Strategic Cooperation Agreement between the two banks in Berlin. The signing was witnessed by Hu Jintao, President of China, on an official visit to Germany, and Germany's President Horst Köhler.

02

03

CHRONICLE

Chronicle

1870, March 10	Deutsche Bank is founded in Berlin as a foreign trade financing bank.
1872, May	Deutsche Bank opens a branch in Shanghai.
1875, October	Deutsche Bank closes its branch in Shanghai.
1889, February 12	Foundation of Deutsch-Asiatische Bank in Berlin by a German bank syndicate led by Disconto-Gesellschaft and Deutsche Bank.
1890, January 2	Deutsch-Asiatische Bank opens its main branch in Shanghai.
1890, December 1	Deutsch-Asiatische Bank opens a branch in Tientsin (now Tianjin).
1897	Deutsch-Asiatische Bank opens an agency in Hankow (or Hankou, now part of Wuhan).
1898, March 17	Deutsch-Asiatische Bank participates in the Chinese Imperial Government Gold Loan for 16 million pounds.
1898	Deutsch-Asiatische Bank opens an agency in Tsing-Tao (now Qingdao).
1899	Deutsch-Asiatische Bank converts its agency in Tsing-Tao into a branch.
1899, June 14	Deutsche Bank and Deutsch-Asiatische Bank assist in the foundation of the Shantung Railway Company.
1900, February 8	Deutsch-Asiatische Bank opens a branch in Hong Kong.
1904	Deutsch-Asiatische Bank opens an agency in Tsinanfu (now Jinan).
1905, July 1	Deutsch-Asiatische Bank opens an agency in Peking (now Beijing).
1907, June 17	Deutsch-Asiatische Bank starts issuing its own banknotes.
1910	Agencies in Hankow and Peking are turned into branches.
1910	Deutsch-Asiatische Bank opens an agency in Canton (now Guangzhou).
1911	Deutsch-Asiatische Bank converts its agency in Canton into a branch.
1913, May 21	Deutsch-Asiatische Bank participates in the Chinese Government Reorganisation Gold Loan for 25 million pounds.
1914, August	At the beginning of the First World War, the Hong Kong branch of Deutsch-Asiatische Bank is closed.

1914, November 10	The Tsing-Tao branch of Deutsch-Asiatische Bank is closed by the Japanese.
1917, August 14	The Deutsch-Asiatische Bank branches in Shanghai, Canton, Hankow, Peking, Tientsin and Tsinanfu are subjected to forced liquidation by the Chinese government.
1924, June 6	Agreement between the German and Chinese governments. Deutsch-Asiatische Bank's buildings are returned.
1925	Re-opening of the Deutsch-Asiatische Bank branches in Shanghai, Hankow, Peking, Tientsin, Tsing-Tao and Canton.
1945, September 27	Deutsch-Asiatische Bank branches in Shanghai, Peking, Hankow, Tientsin and Tsing-Tao are closed.
1945, November 26	Deutsch-Asiatische Bank closes its branch in Canton.
1949, February	Deutsch-Asiatische Bank is licensed as a foreign trade bank in Hamburg.
1953	The headquarters of Deutsch-Asiatische Bank are officially relocated from Shanghai to Hamburg.
1958, October 1	Deutsch-Asiatische Bank re-opens a branch in Hong Kong.
1972, January 6	Foundation of European Asian Bank by an international syndicate led by Deutsche Bank.
1972, November 6/7	The Deutsch-Asiatische Bank branches in Hamburg and Hong Kong are taken over by European Asian Bank.
1974	The Hong Kong branch of European Asian Bank opens its first neighbourhood branch in the city, soon followed by others.
1976, October 18	Deutsche Bank opens a representative office in Hong Kong.
1979, October 8	Deutsche Bank converts its representative office in Hong Kong into a branch.
1981, September 4	Deutsche Bank opens a representative office in Beijing.
1982	Opening of the eighth neighbourhood branch of European Asian Bank in Hong Kong.
1983	Deutsche Bank increases its participating interest in European Asian Bank to 60 per cent.
1986, May	Deutsche Bank increases its participating interest in European Asian Bank to 75 per cent.
1986, November	European Asian Bank becomes Deutsche Bank (Asia).
1987, April	Deutsche Bank AG increases its participating interest in Deutsche Bank (Asia) to 100 per cent.

1988	Deutsche Bank (Asia) is merged into Deutsche Bank AG. The management of the Asia business is relocated from Hamburg to the regional head office in Singapore.
1994, January 1	Deutsche Bank AG opens a representative office in Guangzhou (formerly Canton).
1995, May 10	Deutsche Bank AG converts its representative office in Guangzhou into a branch.
1995, August 17	Deutsche Bank AG opens a representative office in Shanghai.
1999, August 12	Deutsche Bank AG converts its representative office in Shanghai into a branch.
2004, November 2	Deutsche Bank AG converts its representative office in Beijing into a branch.
2005	Deutsche Bank makes a 19.5 per cent strategic investment in local asset management firm Harvest Fund Management – one of the country's leading investment managers.
2006, May	Deutsche Bank acquires a 9.9 per cent stake in Hua Xia Bank.
2006, November	Deutsche Bank's Private Wealth Management business starts to provide onshore financial advisory services to high-net-worth individuals in Shanghai.
2007, March 14	Deutsche Bank launches its Private & Business Clients service in China and opens sub-branches in Beijing and Shanghai.
2007, June	Deutsche Bank and Hua Xia Bank launch joint credit card operations.
2008, January 2	Deutsche Bank (China) Co., Ltd., a wholly foreign-funded subsidiary bank solely owned by Deutsche Bank AG, officially commences operations. The branches and sub-branches of Deutsche Bank AG in Beijing, Shanghai and Guangzhou are converted into corresponding branches and sub-branches of Deutsche Bank China, with headquarters in Beijing.
2008, February	Deutsche Bank increases its stake in China's leading fund management company, Harvest Fund Management Co. Ltd (Harvest), to 30 per cent ownership.
2008, March	Deutsche Bank increases its equity stake in Hua Xia Bank to 13.7 per cent.
2008, April	The Deutsche Bank Tower in the Chao Yang District, Beijing, is officially opened. It is the headquarters of Deutsche Bank (China) and home to the Beijing branch office.

Text

Werner Plumpe, Professor of Economic and Social History at the Goethe University, Frankfurt am Main

Photos

akg-images: 35 (6), 36, 79
Bildarchiv Preußischer Kulturbesitz, Berlin: 33, 58
Deutsche Bank AG, Group Internal Communications: 129
Deutsche Bank AG, Historical Institute: back cover (2, 4), 32, 34, 37 (10), 40–41, 43–46, 48–49, 55–56, 59–70, 78, 80–87, 90–91, 94–97, 100–107, 110–112, 114–121
Deutsche Bank AG, Hong Kong Branch, Communications: 126–127
Deutsche Bank AG, Asia Pacific Head Office, Brand Communications: 113, 123, 125, 128
Deutsche Bank Privat- und Geschäftskunden AG, Communications: front cover, 122, 124
Albert Herrmann, Historical and Commercial Atlas of China, Harvard University Press, 1935, 62–63: endpapers
Frank H.H. King, The Hongkong Bank in Late Imperial China 1864–1902, Cambridge University Press, 1987, illustrations between 280 and 281, no. 9: 37 (11)
Theodor Rehm (personal papers): back cover 1, 47, 51–54
Dr. Reimar Roll, Ernst von Semmern (personal papers): back cover 3, 71, 74–75
SV Bilderdienst (Scherl): 72–73
Ullstein Bild: 50, 92–93
Virtual Shanghai: 35 (7), 42
www.lib.utexas.edu/maps/historical/hankow_1915.jpg: 57

ISBN 978-3-492-05210-8

Layout: R.M.E Roland Eschlbeck/Rosemarie Kreuzer, Munich
Page design: Elisabeth Petersen, Munich
Production: Kösel, Krugzell
Printed in Germany

www.piper.de

O U T E R M O N G
Dzasagt
Tushetu-k
Urun-goza
Pichan
Chên-hsi-fu
Kümul, Hami
Hsing-hsing-hsia
Chü-yen L.
Etzina
Torgut
P'ing-shu-yüan
Alashan
Ölet
Shande-miao
Sudji
Urot
INNE
Tsagan-chul
Wu-yüan
Huang-ho
Pao-t'ou
Kuei-hu
Ting-k'ou
Ordos
Otok
Kishin-bai
An-hsi
Tun-huang
Yü-mên
Kansu
Former boundary
Chia-yü-k.
Mao-mu
Su
Syrtyn-nor
Ulanbulak
Kan-chou
Kao-t'ai
Shan-tan
Chên-fan
Ting-yüan-ying
Yung-ch'ang
Liang-chou
Ning-hsia
Kara-nor
Karluk
Tibetans
Tangut
Dulan-kitt
Ku-lang
Chung-wei
Hua-ma-ch'ih
Yü-lin
Hadjir
Tsohan
Barun-kure
Tenkar
Hsi-ning
Ch'ing-hai, Kuku-nor
Gumbum
Nien-po
P'ing-fan
Ching-yüan
Hai-ch'eng
Huan
Ku-yüan
Ch'ing-yang
Fu
Yen-an
Dichu-rabdan
Kuei-te
Lan-chou
Starry Sea
Djugubu
Mümütan
Lama-tologoi
Ho
Ti-tao
T'ao-chou
Hua-p'ing-ch'uan
Kung-ch'ang
P'ing-liang
Ning
Pin
Golok
Ngamachu
Keguao
Min
Ts'in
Ch'ing-shui
Fêng-hsiang
Wei-ho
Hsi-ho
Li
Ch'êng
Hsi-an
T'ung-chou
Chieh
Wên
Shang
Sung-p'an
Han-chung
Han-chiang
Hsing-an
Riuchi
Chiamdo
Darge-gonchen
Kandse
Mao
Lung-an
Li-fan
CH'IEN-TSANG = ANTERIOR TIBET
Bargo
Lhedjong
Drango
Cucin
Zanla
Mou-kung
Mien
Pao-ning
Sui-ting
K'uei-chou
Namcha-barwa
Showa
Lan-ts'ang-chiang
Nu-chiang, Salween
Pa-an, Batang
Ch'ung-ch'ing
Ch'êng-tu
Szechwan
Shun-ch'ing
T'ung-ch'uan
Wan
Chung
Ya-chou
Mei
Litang
Kang-ting, Ta-chien-lu
Tien-ch'uan
Izu
Shih-nan
Brewa-gomba
Mishmi
Sadiya
Rima
Dibrugarh
Menkong
ASSAM
Chia-ting
(1897)
Hsü-chou
Lu
Ta-chiang
Yu-yang
Yün
Hsien-fêng
Mo
Wei-hsi
Yung-ning
Chung-tien
Ning-yüan
Chao-t'ung
Ch'ih-shui
Tsun-i
Ssü-nan
Sung-t'ao
Kachin
Maingkwan
Irravadi
Li-chiang
Yung-pei
Ya-lung-chiang
Chên-hsiung
Yung-ning
Pi-chieh
T'ung-jên
Ssü-chou
Chên-yüan
Huang-chou
Miao
Ta-ting
Tung-ch'uan
P'ing-yueh
Kuei-yang
Myitkyina
Ta-li
An-shun
Tu-yün
Li-p'ing
Ching
Yün-nan
Teng-yueh, Momein
(1902)
Yung-ch'ang
Mêng-hua
Chü-ching
Tu-shan
I-chia
Yao
Bhamo
Shun-ning
Chu-hsiung
Chêng-chiang
Hsing-i
Kwei-chou
MIEN-TIEN = BURMA
(1886 to British India)
Ching-tung
Chên-yüan
Kuang-hsi
Hsi-lung
Ssü-ch'eng
Ch'ing-yüan
Liu-chou
Chên-pien
P'u-erh
Lin-an
Kuang-nan
Mêng-tzü
(1889)
Kwangsi
Po-sê
Chên-an
Ssü-ên
Hai-chia
Yüan-chiang
Ssü-mao
(1892)
K'ai-hua
Mandalay
Mêng-lien
Lakuis
Ho-k'ou
Lao-k'ai
Kuei-shun
Lung-chou
(1889)
T'ai-p'ing
Nan-ning
Hsün-ch
Kü-lin
Mêng-hun
Songkoi R.
Liang-shan, Langson
Shang-ssü
Ch'in
Lien-chou
Keng-Tung
Mekong
Tung-ching = Tongking
(1885 to France)
Ho-nei, Hanoi
Pei-hai, Pakhoi
(1877)
Lei-chou
Gulf of Tongking
Hsiao-
Hoi-lo
Scale 1:10 000 000
Miles
0 25 50 100 150
Kilometers
0 50 100 200 300